TIBETAN VOICES

A TRADITIONAL MEMOIR

PHOTOGRAPHS BY BRIAN HARRIS

WRITTEN AND EDITED

BY

HEATHER WARDLE,

ELIZABETH CASS,

IAIN MARRS,

AND

GEORGE CSABA KOLLER

POMEGRANATE ARTBOOKS • SAN FRANCISCO

For Margaret and Austin

Published by Pomegranate Artbooks
Box 6099, Rohnert Park, California 94927

Pomegranate Europe Ltd.
Fullbridge House, Fullbridge
Maldon, Essex CM9 7LE, England

Pomegranate Artbooks and Seva would like to thank the publishers for
permission to quote and/or adapt material from the following
publications:

In Exile from the Land of Snows by John F. Avedon, 1994.
HarperPerennial Edition.

Lord of the Dance by Chagdud Tulku, 1992. Padma Publishing.

Princess in the Land of Snows by Jamyang Sakya and Julie Emery, 1990.
Reprinted by arrangement with Shambhala Publications, Inc., 300
Massachusetts Avenue, Boston, MA 02115.

"A Tailor's Tale," recounted to Kim Yeshe by Gyeten Namgyal, 1994,
from *Chö Yang*, Issue No. 6.

Library of Congress Cataloging-in-Publication Data

Tibetan voices: a traditional memoir/photographs by Brian Harris:
  written and edited by Heather Wardle . . . [et al.].
      p.   cm.
    ISBN 0-7649-0020-X (hardcover). —ISBN 0-7649-0004-8 (pbk.)
    1. Buddhism—China—Tibet. 2. Buddhism—Himalaya Mountains
Region.   3. Himalaya Mountains Region—Pictorial works.
4. Buddhism—China—Tibet—Pictorial works. 5. Buddhism—Himalaya
Mountains Region—Pictorial works. I. Harris, Brian, 1951–
II. Wardle, Heather.
BQ7616.T538   1996
951'.5—dc20   96-26458
                                                  CIP

Pomegranate Catalog No. A849

Designed by Bonnie Smetts Design

Printed in Korea
01   6 5 4 3 2

First Edition

[CONTENTS]

PRAYER FLAGS AND CAIRNS, LAKE NAMTSO, TIBET

[FOREWORD]

BRIAN HARRIS

ONE SHOULD NOT TAKE OUTWARD BEAUTY FOR REALITY:

HE WHO DOES NOT UNDERSTAND THIS MYSTERY WILL NOT OBTAIN TRUTH,

EVEN THOUGH HIS PICTURES MAY CONTAIN LIKENESS.

—CHING HAO, CHINESE BRUSH PAINTER, TENTH CENTURY

While traveling in Tibet in 1994, I encountered a family of pilgrims circumambulating a series of sacred mountains in a region west of Lhasa. Their party of eight was being led by elderly twin brothers, each tall and handsome. As we talked, one of the brothers supported his folded arms upon his walking stick; then, resting his head on his arms, he gazed up at me with an expression of kind and curious humor. It was a delightful moment, and I thought it a good time to ask, with the help of my translator, permission to take their photograph. The brothers declined my request. After we had continued on our way, I questioned my translator, Nambu, asking what the reason might be for their refusal, since this had rarely happened. Some elderly Tibetans, Nambu explained, are particularly concerned about having their image recorded because they prefer to have few remains in this world after they have died to keep them tied to their former existence. Also, Tibetans see photographs of people reproduced in newspapers and magazines, lying discarded on the ground, where they are trampled on, perhaps mixed up with garbage in a rubbish heap. This, in the view of some older Tibetans, is a disrespectful and insulting way to treat a person's likeness.

This event brought to mind an insightful essay by Ananda K. Coomaraswamy entitled "The Traditional Conception of Ideal Portraiture."[1] Here Coomaraswamy presented various canonical traditions related to sacred portraiture in both the East and the West. He revealed a common proscription against the representation of human likeness, and, in the words of the *Sukranitisara,* a condemnation of it as not "heavenward leading." My experience in Tibet suggests a sound psychological foundation for this precept and its durability through time.

Perhaps one principle underlying this uneasiness about photographic portraiture is the Buddhist understanding that our human existence is a precious and extremely rare opportunity for spiritual liberation. This principle can lead to natural concern about abusing our human state—even in the form of an exact image of oneself. To a sophisticated modern mind the reactions of traditional peoples to photography may appear to be just a quaint example of simple superstition. However, if we juxtapose this response with that encountered in "developed" societies when our own photograph is taken or we photograph others, the degree of anxiety or self-inflation that many of our contemporaries experience is both astounding and revealing. Whether it is the familiar identity crisis that so many people experience in front of the camera, or the dissatisfaction with what the camera and film produces, the modern and "enlightened" reaction may be more indicative of a fragile and superstitious sense of self than is a calm rejection of photographic portraiture grounded in a deep metaphysical principle. The modern world has forgotten or lost the means of orientation toward its sacred and transcendent center, and this absence has led to a conception of self and other that is limited and thus fragile.

In most situations, however, the people I photographed for this book were content to have their photograph taken without any apparent anxiety. The two images titled *Reciting Prayers in a Monastery Courtyard* and *Muslim Neighbor* (see p. 76) epitomize the natural and self-composed qualities often manifested by traditional people, with or without a camera present.

Another noteworthy response connected with photographic portraiture is the deliberate and idealized presentation of self by Tibetan *lamas,* or spiritual adepts. During certain initiation rites a lama or *yogi* will "transform" him- or herself by embodying (bringing to mind) a particular deity, or *yidam.* Often a visual change in the yogi's facial expression is witnessed as the recollected deity, or the yogi's spiritual essence is manifested for the spiritual benefit of the initiates present. This portrayal of the yogi's true nature stems from an interior contemplative exercise that utilizes visualization, sacred *mantras,* and ritual hand gestures called *mudra.* With the addition of symbolic implements and ceremonial clothing, this exercise transforms the lama into a "living icon." Lamas began to record and extend this "visual benediction" to posterity when the camera was introduced to Tibet in the early years of this century.

Until recently, Tibet itself was, in a sense, just such a living icon, and the diaspora of its people and traditions an auspicious blessing to the world. The contours of Tibet's cultural "soul" were fashioned out of the elemental forces of earth and sky and quickened by the teachings of the Buddha and lineages of monks, nuns, and saints. Tibetan society revolved around a profound metaphysical and cosmological axis. It was a civilization deeply rooted in a sacred worldview. The ultimate and blissful goal for Buddhists is liberation from this and all other realms of impermanence and suffering through the practice of contemplative insight and compassionate or virtuous action. Providentially, Tibet was cloistered high up in the Himalaya Mountains and for the most part was unaffected by modern ideological and technological developments.

During the early years of this century the storytellers within this book were living in a land that had little in common with the world outside its borders and that, up to the occupation of Tibet by the Chinese army in 1959, was a continuation of that of their ancestors. Seventy years ago, few Tibetans suspected—although some prophesied—that they might be the last generation in their country's ancient history.

Tibetan Voices: A Traditional Memoir is a portrait of these last years, or rather a sketch, since the memoirs and photographs published here are but glimpses of what was once a varied and complex society. In spite of these limitations—and the foregoing cautions regarding mirrorlike portraiture—by summoning the powers of imagination, heart, and mind we can discern beyond the surface of these images and stories the profound principles that guided Tibetan society.

Human nature is such that any insight concerning a nation's sacred and religious roots—and their effect on its character—can and does fall only too easily into a comfortable idealization unless we also acknowledge the more down-to-earth aspects of everyday life and human character. Some of the material in this volume may act as a mild antidote to this tendency to romanticize Tibetan society.

Tibet was not a land largely populated by the meek and holy, by people purified of all human frailties and follies. Our storytellers were exceptionally candid when narrating their memories. For example, although we can only include a few of Lobsang Gyaltso's stories, his well-deserved fame for being a great practical joker, despite being the head of an esteemed religious institution, will be confirmed by his stories "Payback" and "The Sleeper Awakes." His pranks were always elaborate and often painful for the unfortunate recipients, and without exception Lobsang's quick and clever mind provided him with a means of escaping retribution or punishment.

Feeding and serving 2,500 monks using Ganden Monastery's immense cauldrons and kettles was never a contemplative or serene task. In Gekoe Lobsang Samdup's recounting of the time he was a kitchen master, he enthusiastically describes how fifty monks were always on hand at serving time, with whips and sticks, to keep order and prevent fights between the servers. In the story "Dob-dob Life," his advancement within the monastery hierarchy was facilitated by winning a communal fight and by surviving the brutal punishment that followed. At every level of society, regardless of who is telling the story, the reader is liable to come upon both an earthy sense of humor and an inclination for impulsive and assertive action. This side of the Tibetan character, along with a fierce determination and clever wit, supports the development of milder qualities such as generosity, patience, and compassion. Just as these attributes were cultivated in traditional Tibet, so they are essential now for Tibetans on both sides of the Himalayas as they encounter the multitude of forces working against their worldly and spiritual liberation.

Tibet has symbolized for many the archetypal holy land that we all seek. A return to old Tibet is impossible, regardless of future developments, but the principles and qualities that were the foundation of Tibet's Buddhist civilization can, at any time and place, be reclaimed.

There is a story recounted within this book that strangely echoes aspects of this search with its inevitable losses and gains. The story is that of a young nomad shepherd on a hillside, far from home, tending his sheep. Suddenly he sees a strange light reflected from something just below the earth's surface. As he nears the light he senses an unusual fragrance. The story that unfolds is a classic tale of treasure found. A portion of the coveted substance is collected and delivered to the nomad community, where it serves its purpose, albeit dwindling with the years. Returning to the source, the young nomad finds that the mother lode has disappeared, reclaimed by its true owner. The community marvels and profits in its disappearance just as it did in its discovery, and the nomads continue on.

—Brian Harris

Ching Hao is quoted in "Pi Fa Chi" (Notes on brush work), in *Chinese on Art Painting* (Siren, n.d.), n.p.

1. Ananda K. Coomaraswamy's essay "Traditional Conception of Ideal Portraiture" is from his book *Christian & Oriental Philosophy of Art* (Mineola, N.Y.: Dover Publications, 1956), 117–27.

PINS AND BRACELETS OFFERED IN RETURN FOR A SHARP MIND AND PROSPERITY, TRANDRUK MONASTERY, TIBET

Two Hermits, Tashi Dorje Hermitage, Lake Namtso, Tibet

Tibetan culture has existed like an endangered species of alpine flower. The conditions that gave rise to this species, and those that sustained it for more than a thousand years, are unlikely to ever occur again.

Given the globalization of materialism, one may wonder what sort of inner worlds existed in a culture that looked on materialism as a bad joke. The Tibetans, with their mountain hardiness and their earthy gaiety, possessed a life-skeptical philosophy. That is, life was seen as a terminal organic process that had to be transcended. The idea of trying to base their deepest values on the survival principle was alien to them.

In looking at the stories and photos that follow, I try to step into another world. To grasp its texture, I attempt to distance myself for a moment from my time and place. I do this because I am a modern, conditioned by a future-oriented rather than a past-oriented culture. Our occidental predisposition is to accept a rupture with the values of the past. The scientific method has given us a type of control over the conditions of life, but at the same time it has eliminated our capacity to infuse life with something beyond life. Technology, as one philosopher has expressed it, is the fulfillment of Western metaphysics.

"Never before has there been such an enslavement through consciousness as in the twentieth century," wrote the Polish poet Czeslaw Milosz. He was referring to our vulnerability to and complicity with ideologies that erode traditional identities and affiliations. As we learn to manipulate the here and now with ever greater skill, our deepest values become aligned with those of survival, and the light of the Beyond fades from view. Many of our social and love relations are carried out in the atmosphere of the will to power. This concept of power underpins our century's vision of life, and it has obvious consequences. The unacknowl-edged grievance at the loss of metaphysical unity has resulted in a virtual renaissance of skepticism.

Many of us can no longer even imagine the atmosphere of a medieval society gripped by an instinct for the absolute. While the popular concept of a medieval theocracy is one of rigid authoritarianism and limited personal liberty, the Western historian Guiseppe Tucci, reflecting on his experience of Tibetan religious culture, understood it more positively: "I loved the medieval aura still enshrouding Tibet and found that, in spite of appearances, it allowed man a greater self-mastery than the Western way of life. The State was not an anonymous tyrant poking his nose everywhere."[1]

What happened to our instinct for the absolute? We have to go as far back as Hegel to find a major Western philosopher still standing on what all medieval philosophers East and West would call familiar ground. Like that of the Buddhist philosophers of Tibet, Hegel's ambition was to illustrate the relationship between the relative and the absolute. He believed that the ideal aim of human awareness was the transcendence of the subject-object division. This transcendence was intimately connected to an uncompromising ideal of personal liberation. Already in Hegel, however, one recognizes a titanic struggle with the emerging modern ethos, an ethos that was unwilling to undertake this task.

To phrase it with ironic simplicity, in the struggle between the subject and the object, the object won. A new age began with a spectrum of ideologies that have tried to justify the dependence of human values on economic realities. From that point on, certain key words such as *revolution, progress, emancipation, development,* and *crisis* become the new foci of what is significant for modern consciousness. They suggest the need to activate something, repair something, gain something. They are resonant with will. There is no serenity in them, no feeling that human life is settled in itself. They are as far as possible from the sense of archaic timelessness and serenity that we experience in the stories and photos in this book.

At this point I could sum up the difference that separates us from that Tibetan world as follows: for us moderns, the "self" has become a problem. We are obliged either to undertake the task of defining ourselves in a spiritual void, or to grope intuitively for the primary forms of selfhood that may lie hidden in the unconscious. In one of the stories that follow, a nomad boy is traded to a noble family from Lhasa and later embarks on a quest. Driven by something undefined in himself, he leaves his new family and becomes an itinerant beggar. His is not a rational process of self-definition; it is an intuitive odyssey. It is a trajectory away from the structured life of upper-class society to the unstructured life of a wanderer and back again. This circular movement of a "self" in search of itself suggests a wholesome outcome to an unconscious conflict.

In "The Begging Classes," however, we find that even the apparently unstructured life was structured. The beggars were highly organized, self-defined, and knowledgeable about their rights. People were in some ways more themselves because they were closer to the archetypes. As one writer described Tibet, the archetypes of the bandit, the princess, the beggar, the monk, the mystic, and the merchant were clearly defined. It is the archetype that provides the basic outline of a character, and in this sense provides self-definition. In "The Opera Singer," there is a noticeable ease in the tone with which the man talks about himself. "I was a very beautiful child," begins the story. As we read on, we feel the speaker's detachment from this "I" that does not seem to bend such special features as beauty into the orbit of the ego. In another case, a man reflects on how as a child he had always built things out of stones and pebbles. He follows his instinct for creating and becomes a master craftsman.

When we encounter this kind of natural unfolding of the "self" in our Western world, it strikes us as an outstanding and beautiful thing. It is like encountering a person who, in his or her momentary crossing of the stage of life, becomes timeless for an instant. Beneath the surface of his or her actions, profundities seem to abound.

The stories and photographs presented here of Tibet and its people capture many of these archetypal features. The landscape itself seems archetypal with its Olympian peaks. The mineral compositions blend natural, human, and supernatural creativities. A pile of rocks may be either a glacial deposit or the site of a prayer. The cairns are stacked on a plain that leans against a horizon that is infinite. A shadow falls from this infinitude, leaving a structure of silhouettes that are frozen in time.

The sky exerts a presence on the landscape that suggests that the heavens are more than just a metaphor for consciousness. The stillness of the hills is like the stillness of the two hermits in front of the temple. There is a transparency that results from the reunion of subject and object that is captured in the imagery of one of Milarepa's songs:

THE ESSENCE OF MIND IS LIKE THE SKY;
SOMETIMES IT IS SHADOWED BY THE CLOUDS OF THOUGHT-FLOW.
THEN THE WIND OF THE GURU'S INNER TEACHING
BLOWS AWAY THE DRIFTING CLOUDS.
YET THE THOUGHT-FLOW ITSELF IS THE ILLUMINATION.
THE EXPERIENCE IS AS NATURAL AS SUN- AND MOONLIGHT,
YET IT IS BEYOND BOTH SPACE AND TIME.

Time is absorbed back into itself, there is nothing happening. Waiting has taken that which it is waiting for and calmed it, digested it.

—Mark Heffernan

1. Guiseppe Tucci, *To Lhasa and Beyond* (Reprint, Ithaca, N.Y.: Snow Lion Publications, 1988), 101.

ACKNOWLEDGMENTS

To the Tibetan elders I interviewed for this book, many of whose stories could not be included because of space limitations, I offer a sincere expression of gratitude. They graciously set aside time from their often demanding daily activities to answer my seemingly endless questions, always offering me the legendary Tibetan hospitality that travelers and foreign friends have come to know and rely on.

Conducting interviews and developing possible story lines within the interview process was at times a tedious and lengthy process. Interviews were conducted in Canada, the United States, Dharamsala, and the Tibetan refugee camps of Ladakh, India. To my translators and guides—Yonten Gyatso, Chimey Singe, Lobsang Yeshe, Pema Youdon, Kunzang Gyaltsen, Tenzin Yeshe, Sonam Chopel, Jhampa Shaneman, Gareth Sparham, Tsepal and Tsezom Yuthok—thank you for your goodwill, patience, and constant concern for accuracy.

I express my deep gratitude to those who knowingly or unknowingly were included in my photographs. I have strived to portray the dignity and depth of beauty so clearly manifest in the Tibetan people and their traditions. In a similar spirit, I offer very special thanks to the Tibetans within Tibet who gave me wise and helpful counsel during my two photographic journeys and the inspiration to undertake the Tibetan Voices Project itself.

One of the most challenging aspects of this project was finding people who had particular experiences and livelihoods while still living in Tibet in the early years of this century. I would arrive out of the blue at a Tibetan merchant's streetside stall in a refugee settlement or a local Tibetan government-in-exile office with a list of life experiences that I was looking for, always adding that I was keen to meet a good story-teller or a person who was well known for talking endlessly about the "old days." Thanks go to those valued community guides. In particular, I want to acknowledge Cynthia Hunt, Betsy Napper, the Departments of Education and of Information and International Relations in Dharamsala, as well as Chokey Tsering and Tsering Zongdho for their help in recording stories in Canada.

Maintaining the authentic voice of our storytellers was of paramount concern in the story creation process. This was achieved by the most expert talents of our writing team: Heather Wardle, Elizabeth Cass, Iain Marrs, and George Csaba Koller. In particular, I would like to thank Iain for his exceptional counsel and assistance during this five-year project. Tsewang Tethong was very kind to proof the text for accurate cultural references, and Tsezom Yuthok spent many hours transcribing interviews in the early stages of this project. A particular expression of gratitude to my friend Mark Heffernan and to Liliana Tomaszewka for their collaborative contribution of a perceptive and sensitive preface. Publishing was a new experience for me, and the folks at Pomegranate have been a joy to work with. A special acknowledgment to Thomas Burke, the president of Pomegranate, and to Jill Anderson and Pat Harris in Pomegranate's editorial department.

This project required constant and prolonged attention, to the point of zealous preoccupation, as my partner, Paula, can surely attest. Her kindhearted support and proofreading talents sustained both myself and the Tibetan Voices Project over the last five years. The project in general could not have been brought to fruition without the generous help and skilled talents of a great many people and organizations. A complete recognition of its supporters and financial patrons would require many pages; thus I apologize for the regrettable but necessary absence of some of their names.

Seva Service Society expresses its accolades and appreciation to the following funders of the Tibetan Voices Project for their generous support and financial contributions: THRESHOLD FOUNDATION, LONDON OPTICAL, ISLAND PAPER MILLS, HEMLOCK PRINTERS, LOWEPRO CAMERA, VIDEO AND COMPUTER BAGS, SNOWFLAKE TRADING CORP. LTD., BANYEN BOOKS, MRS. A HARRIS, MICHAEL FUTRELL, RAFFI, Finlandia Natural Pharmacy, West Coast College of Massage Therapy, Monica Franz: West Side Art Therapy Centre, Videomatica, Viscount Communications & Control Systems, Integrative Healing Arts Clinic, G. King Photo-Colour Ltd., Hanuman Foundation, Amethyst Creations, Naam Restaurant, Nights Publications, Festival Cinemas, The Travel Bug, Rastawares, Wanderlust, Bali Bali, Shared Vision, Gamma Pro Imaging, Inc., Vancouver Film School, Leyline Associates, Webwriters Internet Publishing, Aurora Framing, Kindred Spirit, Vajra Adventure Tours (Sikkim), Julia Zarudzka, Jack Sniderman, Kim Boutelier, Sean Pritchard, J. Patric and Erica Smith, Mark and Sue Cocar, Don and Shanti McDougall, Dr. P. Nash, Mukta Vie, Russell Precious, Matthew Cheng, Dr. Michael Prokopczak, Tim and Sylvia Kerr.

There are many volunteers, from Seva and elsewhere, who have donated their time and enthusiasm to promote and sell the Tibetan Voices publications, raising funds for Seva projects and the three Tibetan refugee programs funded by the Tibetan Voices Project. Their efforts have materially lessened our neighbors' suffering.

Royalties from the sale of the *Tibetan Voices* book and calendar will be used to fund the following:

SEVA PROJECTS: Seva works in partnership with community leaders locally and abroad to help them accomplish goals set by their communities that lead them toward self-reliance. Seva's principal activities abroad focus on the prevention and reversal of blindness in developing countries, particularly India and Nepal, and on economic and community development in the highlands of Guatemala and among the Guatemalan refugees in Mexico.

THE TIBETAN HEALTH EDUCATION ORGANISATION is mandated to immediately meet the most life-threatening health needs of Tibetan refugees in Ladakh, India. It also promotes self-reliance by providing them with the training and infrastructural support they require to meet their own needs in the future.

THE NUNS PROJECT was formed in 1987 to improve the education of Tibetan nuns, recognizing that education is the key to providing these women with the resources they need to become self-sufficient and improve their status within the Tibetan community. A recent focus of THE NUNS PROJECT has been the construction of Dolma Ling Nunnery and Institute near Dharamsala, India.

DELEK HOSPITAL AID FOUNDATION was established to help the Tibetan Delek Hospital in Dharamsala to develop its own financial, educational, and institutional resources. The Tibetan Delek Hospital has forty-five beds and provides care for the Tibetan and local Indian communities of Dharamsala.

SEVA SERVICE SOCIETY
200-2678 West Broadway
Vancouver, B.C. V6K 2G3
(604) 733-4284

SEVA FOUNDATION
P.O. Box 11277
Berkeley, CA 94712-9907
(800) 223-7382

PAINTING THE MONASTERY, LAMALING MONASTERY, TIBET

Two Nuns Laughing, Ganden Choling Nunnery, Dharamsala, India

SNOW DELIVERY

TSERING DOLKAR YUTHOK

Before the Chinese took over our country in 1959, Tibet was a happy place. People were very playful, and I remember a childhood filled with laughter. There was one particular wintertime prank called *khang-khay*, meaning "snow delivery," that we would play just after a snowfall. Everyone was watchful because while we were trying to trick other families and friends, they were trying to trick us. Khang-khay went like this: we would make up a package of delicious sweets, fruits, and sometimes even jeweled ornaments, and amongst these gifts we would hide a fist-sized snowball. This bundle was then wrapped in paper or old clothing and sent off with a family member or servant to be delivered to a particular household. As soon as the messenger had handed it over and was out of the household's reach, he would yell, "This is a snow delivery!" The messenger then ran home as fast as he could, trying to make it back without being caught. If he managed it, then the snow delivery was success-ful, and the other household would be obligated to throw a lavish dinner for the family who sent the snow and for all their friends and relatives. Such a dinner involved hundreds and hundreds of guests. But, if the delivery person was caught before running away, the people of that household would make an enormous amount of *tsampa* (barley flour) paste and smear it all over him—on his clothes, on his face, and in his hair. The messenger would then make his way back home where, of course, we were waiting for his return and to know the outcome. If he returned covered in tsampa paste, then we knew that our snow delivery had failed, that we were not skillful enough, and that we would have to host the dinner banquet for the other household and their family and friends.

So, one way or the other, there was always a banquet. Between trying to trick others and suspecting others of trying to trick us, we stayed very alert during the winter months. Alert, playful, and well fed.

SENIOR AND JUNIOR MONK SITTING IN FRONT OF A DRUM, TSURPHU MONASTERY, TIBET

Meeting My Root Guru

Geshe Tashi Namgyal

I had two uncles on my mother's side. My older brother and I lived with the older one. He was a teacher, and we had to study under his instruction. He was a strict disciplinarian, and as a teacher, he would hit everybody. Every day he would beat us for some reason or other. He was such an abrasive and abusive person that I never liked him, but this turned out to be a blessing, for, as a result, I began to search for another teacher.

When I met the teacher who was to become my *guru*, I became very excited and enthusiastically asked my uncle to allow me to enter the higher class of study. My uncle said no. I might add at this point that I often wished my uncle would fall down dead. Since I had decided that I definitely wanted to study with this other teacher, I told my uncle that I would no longer stay in his house. This angered him greatly, but my older brother and I moved out and I had the freedom to enter the higher class of study.

My teacher was very good indeed. He always demanded and received the greatest personal involvement in his teachings. At the start of each day he would place all our names—there were about twenty of us—in a cup or other vessel, and he would pick out a name at random. That person then had to give an example that best exemplified the teaching of the previous day. When my name came up, I was very excited and gave the best response I possibly could. My teacher was greatly pleased with me. In the course of time, I became very close to him. From the very beginning I knew in my heart that I could truly grow if I were able to remain under his guidance for as long as possible. He was an inspiration to me, and with his guidance I did manage to gain some experience of the *dharma*, the way of the Buddha.

In all of this, I was greatly assisted by my older brother. Because I wanted so much to learn, I would study whatever text I was trying to master not only all day, but all evening and even throughout the night. As I continued my studies, I grew quite thin, and at night I would often fall asleep over the texts. My older brother took over the more menial tasks such as getting the food organized and feeding me. It was because of his kindness that I was able to study so deeply and so thoroughly.

POTALA STAIRCASE, THE POTALA PALACE, LHASA, TIBET

MONASTERY STAIRCASE, TRANDRUK MONASTERY, TIBET

LIFE IN THE POTALA

Ngawangthongdup Narkyid

The Potala is such a huge place it was easy for visitors and newcomers to become lost. I remember, as a young student, how we were teased by the older students in the first few weeks after our arrival there. They'd say, "Now you have been here a month, tell us how many rooms there are in the Potala Palace." At the time we didn't know, so when the older students said, "There are 1, 2, 3, 4 rooms," we didn't understand. "Figure it out," they'd say. What they meant was that there were 1,234 rooms! Eventually I knew exactly how many windows and steps there were in those parts of the Potala that we were permitted to enter. We came to know the number of steps on each staircase from the courtyard to the big gong, and from the gong to the foot of the palace, because of a game we used to play. We would race all the way down the many stairs, then immediately back up to see who could come first. During the daytime this was easy, but at night it was very difficult because we couldn't see anything. We had to remember the exact number of steps or else we'd fall. So, as I ran up the steps in the dark, I'd repeat to myself, "1, 2, 3, 4, 1, 2, 3, 1, 2, 3, 4," counting each of them off.

I entered the Potala as a student in 1942 and after completing six years of study I continued to live and work there as a government clerk. Our school was on the palace's eastern side, across the courtyard from the Dalai Lama's residence. In the winter most of the Potala was very cold since the lower parts of the palace had small windows and walls of stone that were five feet thick. But our school and the part of the Potala where we lived had wide windows—without glass, of course—which let in more sun. In the winter there was no need for heating because we wore heavy clothes. In our classroom we sat in rows on long, rolled-up cushions and, from time to time, our seating positions were rotated so that each could have a turn near the windows. Although we all enjoyed the warmth of the sun, the elderly and those with poor health were particularly advised by the doctors to spend more time by a window.

Not far from our school was a public toilet with about eight long, narrow holes cut into the floor. The waste dropped all the way down to the base of the Potala, at least six stories below—so dark you couldn't see down. At certain times of the year farmers would arrive to take it away for their fields. The ashes from our section of the Potala were put down these holes as well, by sweepers especially assigned to the toilets. This toilet room had a number of windows and it was quite windy in wintertime. We'd squat there, often two students on one hole, with scarves wrapped around our faces and ears, passing waste and talking. When we washed our bodies in the winter, we did that together as well. We'd heat up some water and take turns pouring it over each other. Some people, even old men, would use only cold water to bathe, saying that afterwards they felt warmer.

One of the fondest memories of my life in the Potala are of the many birds who shared our lives. There used to be many pigeons there, until the Chinese army forced people to kill them in 1959. There was also a big owl with a huge head like a cat who lived in the palace, calling "OooOooOoo" throughout the night. But above all there were the large ravens; they would gather together in assembly, almost like human beings, to talk and play and, like us, to compete in different kinds of sports! We played with them a lot. We'd shape small disks from tsampa dough and toss them up in the air for the ravens to catch and eat. Both the students and the ravens liked this sport very much and we all became experts at playing it. Our raven friends would come to our windows at certain times of the day to be fed. Though they didn't let us actually touch them, we could get very close and they would take food from our fingers. Most of the monks and students had a raven friend. Ravens have a great sense of humor, as I learned from one particular resident. He told me that one day a raven brought him a necklace of turquoise and coral and put it on his window ledge!

Also living with us in the Potala was a type of orange duck. These ducks made their nests on the lower front windows. The babies would drop down onto the ground from the window so that their parents could take them to the water behind the Potala. It was the duty of the sweepers to protect these birds—particularly the young babies—from the hawks that soared all around. Carrying a long stick to ward off danger, the sweepers walked alongside the ducklings while the parents followed behind or flew above, calling "anh, anh, anh."

Residents of the Potala were permitted to keep pets, including Lhasa Apso dogs and sometimes a cat. Even students could have an animal, though only if their sponsor permitted it in his living quarters. As in the rest of Tibet, each night all the dogs would be set loose to run free. But at the Potala they didn't bark very much; they seemed to sense, "I should keep quiet here." The Potala was a very quiet place, especially at night, and we could hear the barking of the dogs and all the other noises that came up from the village of Shol at the base of the palace. We heard everything very clearly—the sounds of people playing, as well as their fights and arguments, and, behind it all, the Lhasa River rushing along. From parts of the Potala we could even see what was happening down there. In the winter, people often sat on the rooftops and played a game of dice called *sho*. We heard and saw people singing and dancing, and sometimes we even listened to conversations about lovemaking. One person might say to the other, "Now let's go and sleep together," or someone would try to get his or her partner to hurry up so they'd have more time to enjoy each other.

As well as the constant sound of the wind blowing through and around the Potala, there was the tinkle of thousands of bells that hung everywhere as decorations, mixed in with the distant clang of horse and cow bells from the streets below. Initially it was disturbing, this tinkling twenty-four hours a day, but over time we became used to it. Then there were the sounds of rituals being performed and the sweepers saying prayers—"Om Mani Padme Hum, Om Mani Padme Hum." And there were the students—we could even be heard down in Shol village! At four o'clock in the morning and again at nine in the evening we'd gather and chant loudly. The villagers said they enjoyed listening to us, and that our chanting had a very pleasing melody.

There were big gongs at the Potala, and every evening at seven o'clock a gong would sound. This meant that anybody who wanted to leave the palace should set off, and anyone who wanted to enter should come in. After ten minutes the gong would sound a second time, and then we'd have to hurry! After a further ten minutes the gong would be struck a third time and immediately all doors would be closed. Nobody could enter or leave until the next morning! Women never stayed inside the Potala at night, though in the daytime they carried water, food, and various supplies to the apartments. Of course, women would visit and come to the palace on pilgrimage, but officials who were married had a duty to stay alone in the Potala. They could visit their families in Shol and elsewhere, but wives could not live in the palace. Even the Dalai Lama's family lived outside the Potala.

Beggars came to the Potala as pilgrims whenever they wanted. If we saw a visiting beggar who asked quietly, "Please give something," then we might give alms, but public begging was not allowed. Anybody could come to the Potala on pilgrimage from ten o'clock in the morning until four or five o'clock in the afternoon. There were no guards. It was the sweepers and managers of the different sections of the Potala who were responsible for making sure people didn't go into areas closed to the public. If a person was found straying, then a sweeper would approach him and quietly say, "Did you lose your way? Please, not that way. This way, I'll help you," and he would guide them along. Each entrance to the Potala had a gatekeeper who opened and closed the gate and who

PILGRIM RECEIVING BLESSED TEA, GANDEN MONASTERY, TIBET

answered people's questions. Each gatekeeper lived in a small room right beside the gate and would sit on a cushion outside his little shelter, saying prayers or turning a large *mani* prayer wheel.

Occasionally local farmers arrived with whatever fresh produce they might have that month. Never speaking loudly or hurrying, they would walk around selling their goods, perhaps saying quietly, "Fresh radish, fresh radish." Since the Potala did not have any shops, we either acquired what we wanted from these sellers or went down to the village to buy our daily needs. I remember we always eagerly awaited the broom vendors, who sold really beautiful brooms made from grass. Sellers didn't come often, but when they did perhaps two would arrive together, each with small things for sale, never anything too big. They would always know just where to go to sell their wares quietly.

[MANI STONE MAKER]

DR. TROGAWA RINPOCHE

As a child, when we made the circumambulations around Lhasa, I remember seeing mani stone makers all along the route. They carved rocks and slabs of stone and as they worked they would recite the Om Mani text, either in part or in full, or other Buddhist prayers. I realize now that they must have had great perseverance to do this work, though at the time I thought little about it.

There was a very great meditator in Tibet who died during my lifetime. He was the father of a monk who studied with me, my religious brother, who was also a very accomplished meditator, though he had a fierce temper. The father spent his time meditating in seclusion. If people came to see him, he would cease his deeper meditation and begin to carve mani stones and to recite "Om Mani Padme Hum." In this way, neither would he be oblivious to his visitors nor would he discontinue his meditation entirely. A time came when we heard that he had become unwell, and later we learned that he had died. His body was kept for cremation or whatever appropriate ritual. A lama was brought from a monastery to perform the ritual prayers and the *powa* (consciousness transference) ceremony, a duty performed only by highly skilled lamas. But the chosen lama said that the deceased did not need the ceremony because he was already an enlightened being. Accordingly, one butter lamp was lit and placed in front of the stone carver's body, and his body was left lying in state for another week. In the Buddhist tradition, monks and lamas perform *pujas*, or prayer ceremonies, all day and all night beside the corpse.

As people walked by to pay their last respects, they noticed that in the air above the body there were rainbow-colored shapes like the patterns on a peacock feather. Over the course of a few days, these floating colors continued to emanate from the body. After four or five days people tried to move the body, but apart from the clothing, which remained like a shell, there was no body left. One of the lamas present said that the body was clearly that of a highly enlightened being. He stated that in this kind of a situation, before the wrappings could be opened, a temporal or secular officer must be informed and invited to the ceremony. The chief was unable to attend, but a representative of the district was sent in his stead. Many other people from neighboring areas came to witness the event. They watched as the coverings that had wrapped the body were removed. Only the carver's hair, fingernails, and toenails remained. That shows the strength of his meditation practice.

MANI STONE CARVER, LAKE REWALSAR, INDIA

MANI WALL, KORZAK VILLAGE, LAKE TSO MORARI, LADAKH, INDIA

Mountain of Mani Stones

Jamyang Sakya

In eastern Tibet, where I was born, there was a place near Singdze that was famous for its white, flat stones. Every day people would go there to collect stones, and some even used oxen to haul the rocks away. But no matter how many stones were taken, there were still many more left. In Singdze itself there were perhaps one hundred families, all of whom made a living carving mani stones—carving prayers and symbols on these white stones and then painting them. Some bore the mantra "Om Mani Padme Hum" (Hail to the jewel in the lotus)—hence "mani" stones—while others had long prayers together with all the names of the Buddha and the *bodhisattvas*. If you wanted a long prayer carved, it could take several months, and you might ask more than one family to carve the longer prayers. People sometimes gave the carvers money but more often they gave things like yaks, barley, butter, horses, and cloth. If someone had passed away, it was very beneficial to give that person's clothing and jewelry to the carver as payment.

Near Singdze there was a *gyanamani*, a huge wall of mani stones about two miles long, the largest in eastern Tibet. Many pilgrims whose families had been struck by sickness or death went there. In the center there was a big temple with two special mani wheels known as the hundred-million-prayer wheels because of the multitude of prayers written on paper that each one contained. These prayer wheels each weighed about two tons and required two or three people pulling on huge metal rings to turn them. People circumambulated the wall and when they reached a prayer wheel they would help each other to turn it, perhaps three or four times, and then they would go round the mani stones again.

When mani stones were added to the wall, they weren't just put on top or randomly here and there. There was a special consecration ceremony by monks or lamas after which the stones were placed carefully in a certain spot. I remember once seeing about ten men standing on top of ladders and women at the bottom, passing the mani stones up. All the while the group chanted prayers until they had passed the entire *sutra* up to the top of the wall and placed the mani stones in order.

My hometown was about thirty miles away in Gaba Province. Once my aunt took me with her when she made one thousand *koras*, or circumambulations, around the mani wall. A lama had told her she should do this for her health. I remember it very well because it was fun to do, though my aunt was a very fast walker and I couldn't keep up with her. She would get up at five o'clock in the morning and go around and around, come home, have a break, and then walk around the mountain of stones again until dark. This white wall, made up entirely of mani stones, was three stories high and over a hundred meters deep, and it ran parallel to the Dza River for two miles. I don't know how many thousands of stones there were, but it was huge! When you were far away from it the wall looked beautiful, like a little mountain. When the Chinese Communists came they took all these white rocks and they made bridges with them! It was all destroyed, though I understand that the people are starting to build it again, little by little.

SUNRISE ACROSS THE BRAHMAPUTRA RIVER, SAMYE MONASTERY, TIBET

ROLLING HILLS IN THE DISTRICT OF TSANG, TIBET

DOCTOR PREPARING MEDICINE, ALCHI VILLAGE, LADAKH, INDIA

MEDICAL EXAMS

DR. YESHE DHONDEN

I began to study traditional medicine when I turned eleven, at Lhasa's central medical college, Mendzekhang. Even though my monastery was required to send a bright student each year for medical studies and I was selected, this was my personal choice and not due to pressure from anyone else. Until age twenty-two I studied hundreds of texts, especially the four central tantric texts. Success in pursuing the study of these texts and becoming a scholar depended entirely on the personality of the student. I always followed what my teachers taught, thoroughly and exactly, and I was particularly skilled at memorizing. Even today I can remember and recite these old tantras.

The college routine was quite spartan, but I never complained. At four each morning a bell sounded in the main temple at the head of the courtyard. I had a few minutes to wash and roll up my bedding before hurrying to my classroom to begin memorizing by the soft light of butter lamps. As the mind was believed to be most fresh upon waking, the first three hours before sunrise were given over to the memorization of the 1,140 pages of the four medical *tantras*, the root texts, preached by the Buddha, which, together with hundreds of commentaries and pharmacological catalogues, were the basis of Tibetan medicine. At seven o'clock the instructors quizzed us on the morning's work, after which we would return to our rooms for the day's first bowl of tea.

In school, I was a very reserved boy and didn't do much talking, let alone have the stomach for fighting; I was always shy and very quiet. The others would always say to me, "You're like a nun." Students often fought, but I always stayed to one side and never got mixed up in it. If two people were fighting and one asked me if they were right, I'd say, "Yes, you are right." Then, if the other person asked, "Am I not right?" I would answer ,"Yes, yes, you are right." I agreed with everybody. If there was a fight between those studying to be government officials and the medical students, I was the first to disappear. That's why I was given the nickname *ani*, or "nun."

On the first day of my text recitation examination, I had to go before the teachers and recite the material I had memorized. A student's ability and success at memorization were a matter of dignity. Three tantras were not usually recited at one time. Instead the student might memorize one text one year and recite it at his test, then recite the second tantra the second year, and the third in the third year. What I and some of my friends did was recite all three tantras in one day; in this way our prestige was increased.

The final examination that tested our knowledge of the texts took place in our last year of college. The exam took the form of a traditional religious debate with the clapping of hands and other dramatic movements and postures and took many hours to complete. I challenged each partner with a particular aspect of our studies and he had to answer; he would then ask me about a topic and I had to answer. We stood in front of over two hundred students, with the teacher at one side making notes on our performance and the students asking question after question.

Another test, repeated every other year, was the recognition of the plants that were used to make medicine. First we had to identify each plant and give its qualities. One by one we went through them, improving each time we were tested. I remember one year when some of us had very similar marks, and we were retested—this time with our eyes covered—and told to identify the plants purely by taste and smell. This was very difficult, but fortunately all of us were able to answer correctly.

When the test was over, it was announced that I had come in number one. Later, though, I found out that there had been a catch. Because I was graduating, my friends had pretended to make little mistakes. In reality I was number three, but thanks to their trick I was chosen as the best student in the college.

In these tests there were literally a thousand items laid out for the student to examine—branches, leaves, flowers, roots, and assorted cuts of various woods. There were plants used in the preparation of medicine, as well as those not to be used, and we had to pick the right ones. All plants are useful in some way, but in these tests we had to differentiate between what is used in medicine and what is not. A similar examination on different seeds and minerals was held at other times during the course of our study. Most of the seeds used came from India, and the minerals tested ranged from diamonds and precious stones to iron, brass, and other metals.

We had to remember that each plant has its own essence and its particular uses. When going through them, we had to give each plant's essence, regardless of its usage. For example, there are three types of garlic. One type has a single root, another has three roots, and the last one has many. Also, there is a black and a white, a male and a female garlic. Not all types of garlic are used in medicine, so we had to know the differences, since all the different types of garlic were spread out on the testing tables—with one here, another type further down, and everything all mixed up. We had just fifteen minutes or so to identify all these plants. I was always very relaxed because we worked with these plants every day. But some students, though they knew the plants, made mistakes because they were nervous and hurried their answers. Also, a few students memorized the names of the plants in exactly the same order as they appeared in the texts. As they went around identifying two hundred plants, these students would recite the names in the same order as they had learned them, getting some right but most wrong.

Two tents were set up on either side of the testing area. The students to be quizzed were kept in the one above the testing tent and were called one by one to take the examination. After the test, they were sent down to the second tent, which was farther away. During the examination, two monitors went around with us, to make sure there would be no cheating. They were students from the class who had already finished. Two were needed, in case one happened to be a friend of the student being tested. After we went to the second tent there was no contact between the untested students and the students who had finished the exam. Someone would then yell out that the one being tested had got this many right and this many wrong, so that the students still waiting could tell how everyone was doing. There was never any cheering or other audible reaction because everyone was so tense and serious, waiting for his own turn to come.

My happiest times were spent in nature, going up into the mountains to collect medicinal plants. We didn't have to carry our own bags or belongings because the government provided us with people to take care of everything. Collecting the plants wasn't difficult, either—we just had to walk and our assistants did the picking. The only thing we had to do was find and identify the plants, while they did the gathering. We usually went on these trips in April or May and stayed for about a month. I didn't have to think about anything—just eat, sleep, and collect plants. Arriving in the areas where the nomads lived was like entering paradise—it was so peaceful. The nomads would give us their best curds and cheese. These journeys into the mountains were like a celebration or a festival for us.

I can truthfully say that I suffered only once while collecting plants. That particular year there was a lot of rain and hail, and one evening some other students and I were caught in the forest during a storm, so we missed our dinner. This was the one time we suffered and it wasn't much! As for studying and memorizing texts, this was not very difficult for me even though the Tibetan medical system, and Tibetan philosophy in general, is very deep and sometimes impenetrable.

Eventually, when I was fully qualified to practice medicine, the government provided me with everything I needed: horses to take me where I had to go, porters to carry my belongings, and anything else that I required to reach my destination. Since I was a doctor with a government letter, when I arrived at a monastery I was exempt from the tasks normally required of other monks such as cooking, washing, and cleaning. The doctor just had to read the scriptures and treat his patients. However, not long after I had finished my studies and begun practicing medicine, the Chinese arrived. I heard more and more stories about the killings and about our country's many problems, and my mind was greatly disturbed.

[A TAILOR'S TALE]

GYETEN NAMGYAL

When I was young, Lhasa was still a small city surrounded by parks, lakes, and wooded areas. People liked to go to the Kyichu River and enjoy themselves, eating, playing games, and swimming. Each park had a name. Our family house was in the Torgyalinka Park and we were known as the Torgyaling family. My playmates poked fun at me and asked why I was named after a park.

My father always believed that I was lucky. It is a custom in Lhasa to mark a baby's first outing with a visit to the Jowo statue housed in the Jokhong Temple. After requesting the statue's blessing, my father put me down on the ground and prostrated three times. When he picked me up he found a piece of coral in my hand. It was the kind used as an ornament for the top of hats and it is considered a sign of luck. My parents were overjoyed by such an auspicious omen.

My father taught me to read and write, and began teaching me to sew when I was eight. I learned very quickly, and my first feat was sewing a *tonga*, or monk's shirt. Someone had brought it to my father for stitching, and I picked it up and began to work on it. My father was afraid I would ruin it, but I looked so sure of myself, he let me have my way. Tongas at that time were not what they are today. They had brocade pieces sewn into the front, and making them required special skills. My father was very proud that I executed the work faultlessly. After that, he took me with him everywhere on sewing trips, and I sat at the end of the line of tailors, assisting the elder ones in sewing edges. This was a tedious but important job that beginners had to master.

When I was ten, my father was called to make appliqué *thangka*s of the Sixteen Arhats (*arhat*s are completely enlightened saints) for a high-ranking lama. We used very beautiful brocades. I was the youngest tailor and again I sat at the end of the line. When we had made all the thangkas of the arhats, the lama said that the main thangka, which represented the Buddha, was very important and that he didn't mind wasting material to attain perfection. He ordered that each of the eight tailors present make a Buddha's face, saying he would choose the best among them. Being so young, I was not counted among the tailors and my father asked if I could take his place, explaining, "This child is very special. He won't make it worse than me and we may get a surprise." My Buddha's face turned out to be the best and was selected for the thangka.

I also accompanied my father on his tent-making jobs. Tents were very popular in Lhasa and were used by the aristocrats and wealthy merchants when they had picnics. They were pitched at specific times in the parks surrounding Lhasa. The Tsetrunglingka Park was the main picnicking spot

FABRICATING A LARGE APPLIQUÉ THANGKA, DHARAMSALA, INDIA

CENTRAL SECTION OF A LARGE APPLIQUÉ THANGKA, DHARAMSALA, INDIA

for high officials, and for seven to ten days they would take up residence in a special pavilion. The officials pitched their tents on the roof or around the pavilion and entertained their friends. The arrangements were very elaborate, with carpets and tables spread out and beautiful thangkas hanging on the walls. In the early 1920s, the tents were still made of felt and most were round, in the Mongolian style. They were very heavy and hot in the summer. My father devised a new style, with doors and windows, made of white cotton. They were heavily decorated with appliquéd patterns, in cotton or brocade, and instantly became popular. All the Lhasa tailors were soon busy making such tents and I practiced my stitches on the borders.

I often went with my father to Drepung Monastery to see Demo Rinpoche. One day when I was twelve, and we were on our way to receive a long-life initiation, I suddenly noticed a magnificent array of buildings above Drepung. The walls were white and the roofs glittered with gold. In the middle was a three-story *stupa,* and people were circum-ambulating it. I couldn't understand what this stupa was—it certainly wasn't Drepung, Sera, or Ganden. I pointed to it and asked my father. He looked in the direction I indicated and stared incredulously at the empty sky before him. He admitted he couldn't see anything and promised to ask Demo Rinpoche about it. Demo Rinpoche laughed. He said I had seen the fields of great bliss and advised that I go and beg for tsampa from as many households as I could. Rinpoche was very eccentric and, as a young child, I couldn't imagine behaving so boldly, so I never followed his advice.

About that time, friends of my father noticed my skills and told him that it would be a waste to keep me at home. They suggested that he register me in the Sokhang, the tailors' guild, and see if he could enter me in the government tailoring unit, where I could further my skills through higher training. At that time, all tailors in Lhasa had to register with the Sokhang or be barred from work. When I was young there were seven hundred registered tailors in Lhasa. The most highly skilled among

them formed an elite of one hundred and thirty who fulfilled all the government's tailoring needs. All the tailors wore a *boto,* the round yellow hat shaped like half a grapefruit that indicated government service.

When I was young, the Sokhang sent a petition to the Dalai Lama asking for a raise in pay. The Tibetan cabinet, or Kashag, decreed that, though the government could not pay the tailors more, they would establish a private tailor's tax that would be used to cover the salaries of the government tailors. It was payable each year in December. Registration was compulsory, and failure to register was punishable by ten lashes of the whip. The rule was enforced by the tailors themselves. I remember being sent around Lhasa to try and spot undeclared tailors, who could be identified by needles stuck into the lapel of their *chuba* or bits of brocade thread sticking to the wool of their clothes.

The year I entered the Sokhang there were twelve other tailors on the list. Since my father was the secretary, it was simple for him not only to enter my name, but to put it at the top. New tailors had to do many chores, but my father arranged to have someone else do mine. The apprenticeship of a tailor proceeded in very precise stages. Just learning to hold the needle took about four months, during which time the novice practiced sewing hems and edges. Hand sewing was a highly developed skill, and a good tailor could hand stitch as many as eight shirts a day. Masters developed speed and quality in their pupils by grouping them into small units of five or six students and organizing competitions to detect the fastest and neatest among them. The senior apprentice slapped the ones below him, so there was a very strong drive to stay on top. One day, I came in second in a speed competition and got a black eye. Realizing the danger, masters discontinued face slapping, and instead we had our wrists slapped with bamboo sticks.

When he looked at the work of beginners, the master counted out the stitches that were well done to make his apprentice feel that every stitch mattered. Under this system, our handiwork became fast and fine.

If bad work was presented to the master, he wouldn't utter a word. Instead he'd let out an exclamation of disgust and discard the piece with a look of revulsion. The other tailors would then pick it up, pass it around, and comment loudly on its faults. Finally, the master would take it up and explain to the humiliated apprentice how to improve.

Precious and ancient brocades were the principal material used by members of the Sokhang, but apprentices were made to practice their sewing and cutting on cheaper materials for a long time before they were allowed even to touch the precious fabrics. Master tailors had to use all their skills to carefully plan the use of brocades in order to achieve the best result with the least possible material. Once the basic principles were mastered, a tailor could employ his skills in any field of tailoring. A good tailor could stitch a superb appliqué thangka or cut and sew comfortable, well-fitting clothes for a person of any size or shape.

My father knew the personal tailor of the Thirteenth Dalai Lama. I had always said that I wanted to serve His Holiness, so my father arranged to have me work with this monk, Thupten, who made all of the Dalai Lama's clothes. Nowadays, one can approach the present Dalai Lama and have an ordinary conversation with him. At the time of the Thirteenth, this was unthinkable, because everyone was terribly afraid of him. The Thirteenth Dalai Lama wore Mongolian-style robes and changed his clothes every day. We made red, yellow, and saffron robes out of the most elaborate brocades and, though he wore them more than once, he would never wear the same robe two days in a row. His entourage viewed the clothes he wore as indicators of his mood. If they were red, it meant he was in a fiery mood and you had to be extra careful. If you dared to look at him directly, he would glare back, and you would never try looking again.

The first time I saw the Dalai Lama was when he came through the workshops to give the annual gift of silver coins to the tailors. He was not very tall, but he was imposing in his golden brocade robe. After that, I often saw him when he visited the sewing rooms. He walked around among the tailors, who sat cross-legged on their cushions, their heads bent over their work. The Dalai Lama watched them cutting and scrutinized every detail of their work. If he noticed something wrong, he would scold the tailors, all of whom were wary of his fiery temper.

During my apprenticeship I still accompanied my father on sewing trips and we often went to prepare ceremonial attire for Demo Rinpoche. One day, my father and I were sitting and sewing together. I was embroidering the eyes on the Rinpoche's boots when I saw my father fall over, the brocade still in his hands. Demo Rinpoche bent over to touch my father and we realized that he was dead.

My father's sudden death left us all unprepared, and my mother was particularly shocked. I was only seventeen and my youngest brother was barely walking. My mother decided that I should take over as head of the household and look after the family, since I could earn a good living. In addition to my salary from the government, I was well rewarded for private work and was beginning to be hired to make brocade thangkas, tents, and temple decorations. My mother arranged my marriage to a girl from a good family who lived nearby.

In 1933 the Dalai Lama died quite suddenly. We had heard earlier that he wasn't very well, but it didn't strike me as very significant, as he often had colds. Not long before his death I was busy making an initiation costume for the Kalachakra initiation from a very beautiful white brocade, when His Holiness came into the workroom, looked at my work, and asked me if it would be ready soon. I answered that it would. He nodded his head and I watched him walk slowly away. He was alone, as he often was on these visits to the workshops. It was the last time I saw him. Though he was never to use the costume, our present Dalai Lama wore it when he gave the Kalachakra initiation in Lhasa.

The announcement of the Thirteenth Dalai Lama's departure for the pure lands was made in Lhasa at night. I was sewing in my house when I heard people shouting outside, calling for mourning, ordering that all prayer flags be lowered, that men unwind their hair and women remove their ornaments. From that day the tailor workshops were empty. No one gave orders and gradually the place became deserted, until plans for a golden stupa were put forward and instructions were given to the Sokhang.

Eighty of the one hundred and thirty tailors of the Sokhang were selected to make the brocade decorations for the stupa, which was to be placed in the Potala, near the mausoleums of the other Dalai Lamas. We made an elaborate ceiling frieze using Russian brocades, which were among the finest available. To the east and west of the stupa was a floor-to-ceiling brocade curtain with large representations of sixteen dragons, which stood for the Sixteen Arhats, eight facing from each side. We were given an extraordinary brocade of a single dragon, which had been used as a carpet. Since we couldn't bear to cut it, we decided to use it as a canopy to line the ceiling. Hanging these decorations required a lot of climbing and walking on scaffolds. Since I was young and light-footed, I did most of it. The entire decoration of the room was completed in thirteen days.

It took about one year to construct the stupa and preserve the Dalai Lama's remains. The mummifying process was done at the Potala in the traditional manner, using salt to extract all the body fluids. After the drying was completed, the remains were covered in gold and placed inside the golden stupa. Fourteen people were allowed inside, and I was fortunate to be one of them, being assigned to arrange the robes. Just before the remains were dressed, someone noticed that a protrusion in the shape of an Avalokiteshvara statue, the Buddha of compassion, had naturally emerged from the Dalai Lama's shoulder. This caused quite a stir, and all fourteen lamas and officials filed into the stupa to see it. I was lucky to catch a glimpse of it before it was covered.

The outside of the stupa was elaborately decorated with jewels, gold, coral, turquoise, and *dzi*. Many officials donated the long earrings they wore in their left ears, and these were set at regular intervals into the stupa. I had just bought a new earring, or *sojin*, which was very beautiful and which I proudly wore on special occasions. A tray was brought forward, and when I saw all the sojin lying on it, I thought mine was more beautiful than the rest and deserved to ornament the stupa. I ran home to get it and add it to the others. Since I was present during the construction work, I was able to make sure my sojin was placed where I wanted it, first on the right on the front of the stupa.

When the work on the stupa was completed, I was summoned to Phembo, a day's journey north of Lhasa, to make a *kyigu* for the monastery there. A kyigu is a huge thangka, several stories high, that is hung outside monasteries on special occasions. While I was making the kyigu, a messenger arrived from Lhasa asking me to return immediately because I had just been awarded the title of *chenmo,* or "great one." Among the tailors there were three other masters, or chenmos, at the time, but they were quite old and did not do much active work. The title had been awarded to me in recognition of my skill in private work and on the stupa, which had impressed my superiors. I was only twenty-two.

I was awarded the title at an auspicious ceremony at the main Sokhang office. All my colleagues came to offer me lucky white scarves. After the ceremony, I went home, where all my friends and relatives did the same. Then I went to pay my respects to Reting Rinpoche, who received me in his house in Lhasa. Rinpoche told me that I had served the Dalai Lama well, that the new incarnation would soon be coming to Lhasa, and that I would also be serving him. This made me feel very happy.

When I was twenty-four, my wife died in childbirth. The baby was also lost, and the whole family was deeply unhappy. My mother, who was very religious, felt that we should all stop thinking of worldly things and dedicate our lives to the Buddhist teachings. We all decided to become monks and nuns. My mother gave up all her possessions, including our lovely house in Torgyalingka Park, which she donated to the government. I remember seeing my mother remove her ear ornaments as she prepared to leave for a nunnery, where she spent many years in seclusion.

I took my vows at Ganden, where I was given a new name, Gyeten Namgyal, the one I am using now. My mother had advised me to resign from my post as chenmo and to live a religious life, but I found it difficult to do this immediately. The government had decided to repair and renovate the temples at Samye Monastery, and I was appointed to lead the party of tailors to restore and remake all the temple decorations. I felt an obligation to fulfill this order and promised my mother that I would resign when it was completed.

However, before I could keep my promise, a much bigger project was proposed. It was decided that something had to be done about the two huge kyigus that were displayed in front of the Potala Palace during the Tsongcho Sebang Festival at the end of the second month of the Tibetan year. The largest of the two old kyigus was much too long, since it was originally made to be displayed right down over the steps of the Potala. This was later judged to be unsuitable, and when the kyigu was displayed, the lower part was rolled up so that the protector deities depicted at the bottom were never seen. Both kyigus were extremely weathered, and some of the figures no longer had faces.

One kyigu was thirteen stories long and the other one was nine. To be inspected, these two masses of brocade were unrolled outside in the presence of the cabinet, all the master tailors from our guild, including myself. In these monumental works of art, the eyes of the main deity were the length of a forearm and the deity's face was ten feet high. The cabinet ministers walked up and down along the kyigu's edges, asking the master tailors what they thought. Because of my experience with kyigus, they asked for my opinion, but I chose to remain silent because I didn't agree with another chenmo's ideas on restoration and it would have been improper to disagree publicly with such an elderly and experienced tailor.

After this assembly the cabinet chose to restore the two old kyigus. But before the process began I was summoned and asked why I had said nothing that day. I told the minister, Temba Jamyang, that I thought these kyigus were too old and fragile to withstand repairs and that, for all the work it took, it would be better to make new ones. Temba Jamyang was a man of vision, and the idea of a grand undertaking pleased him. He gave me his approval and put me in charge of the project.

For making the kyigus, forty boxes of material were delivered to us from China, each containing ten or eleven rolls of a very rich brocade, and fifty boxes of plain brocade from Tashilhunpo Monastery in Shigatse. We had to write down each quantity and make an official receipt. The final count was 7,863 squares. I chose sixty tailors from the Sokhang to do the work, and we set up our workshop in the Shol printing press at the foot of the Potala. The largest of the new kyigus was to be the more manageable size of about nine stories tall. The layout was planned in the large grounds near the printing press, using chalk drawings and paper models. Painter Tsering-la was put in charge of making the designs, and I remember that he had a very annoying way of sketching elaborate details, taking hours and hours at a time. The work was not progressing, and I argued that for a work of this size the designs needed to be large. Neither of us would give in, but eventually Tsering-la was replaced by a more cooperative painter, and we were soon able to sketch every figure, cut the brocade, and distribute the work.

The material used to line kyigus was Assam silk, which is known for its strength. I couldn't imagine how we were going to find the necessary two thousand squares without delaying all the work, so we decided to use the old lining and repair the most worn pieces.

The kyigus took eight months to complete. Half of the brocade we were given was left over; the remainder was used to make a new set of costumes for the grandest and most colorful festival of all, the Tsongcho Sebang. The original costumes dated back to the time of the Fifth Dalai

VILLAGERS CONSTRUCTING AN APPLIQUÉ THANGKA, PUNGDA VILLAGE, TIBET

Lama and were in shreds, some nearly beyond recognition. Since no one was around to provide us with details, we took torches and examined the murals in the Potala representing the early processions, and based the new costumes on the lively and detailed paintings. The work took two months and was finished on schedule. It was all such an elaborate affair that people began calling the festival "showing off time."

On the appointed day, the thirtieth of the second month, all the monks and lay government officials lined up in front of the Potala to view the kyigus and take part in the festival. The festival procession waited at the Yuthok Bridge while the new Dalai Lama, still a child, watched from his palace. The curtain that hung behind the kyigu was already in place, and the timing was such that the festival procession would start to move and the kyigus would be unfurled simultaneously. Hanging the kyigus was a massive engineering feat, especially if the wind were high, in which case it would be an extremely dangerous task. I was very much aware of this, since all the tailors had to be present at the foot of the Potala, needles and thread in hand, in case of some mishap. Frankly, I could never understand what good our needles would do in the event of a sudden gust of wind, but we stood on guard, ready more to duck than to sew. The hanging of the kyigus was accomplished by workers in the Potala, all of whom were clad in white chubas and Mongolian hats. The procedure looked like a frightening experience. The workers were roped around their waists and had to hang out of the high windows of the palace to secure all the ropes and attachments.

In the end, I never kept the promise to my mother. I tried to resign from my post as chenmo, but with the arrival of the new Dalai Lama at the Potala, they needed my services. I remained both a monk and a tailor and served the Fourteenth Dalai Lama until His Holiness went into exile.

MASTERING METAL WORK

PEMA DORJE

To amuse myself as a child, while looking after my family's animal herds I used to dig for clay in the ground and make animal or human forms out of it. I kept many of these clay statues on the porch of our house, where people admired them and said how lifelike they were. I particularly liked one of them, the figure of an old man. He was very old, without teeth or hair, and when he slept he would just blow because he had no teeth. He would often come with me when I went to look after the animals. We liked each other very much!

A horoscope had been cast for me at the time of my birth that said I would achieve fame and success if I were allowed to pursue some kind of craft. Nevertheless, my farming family was quite surprised to see me at an early age demonstrate a talent for clay modeling and drawing, since there was no history of these skills in the family. Everyone thought that it would be very good for me to work with the animals because I had an aptitude for making harnesses and other equipment for our horses, donkeys, and yaks. I made saddles, straps, ropes, and leads, and this was considered to be a very helpful and important contribution to our household. But my real interest lay elsewhere.

There was a teacher of metal sculpture near my village who had many students, and I used to go quite often to his house to watch the younger students do their preparatory drawings. I would copy these boys, and people said I drew better than they did even though I had received no training. So my family decided that, because of the strong karmic connection demonstrated by my talent and my innate liking for the craft as well as by the horoscope's indications, I should be allowed to study it. At the age of fourteen, I began to study metal sculpture.

My first teacher was Zamla Dorje, with whom I studied for ten years.

When I first became an apprentice along with sixteen other students, I was like the longest finger—I stood out as the best one. First we were taught how to draw the image of the statue we were going to make, then how to draw diagrams showing all the correct proportions. Next we were taught how to emboss with a chisel and how to make a clay model for the statue. Craftsmen usually specialized in some aspect of their work, so after ten years, when I had learned everything I could from my first teacher, I spent two years studying with the master Chola Shilo, who was renowned for his skills in embossing, and another two years with Dhembu Chola Eunghe, who was famous throughout Tibet for his drawing. After fourteen years under these three eminent masters I felt confident that I could not only create statues of deities in their peaceful and tantric forms, but also teach my skills.

While I was still an apprentice, I was assigned to work on a large order commissioned by the government when the Fourteenth Dalai Lama was expected to be reincarnated. Three thousand statues were to be constructed—one thousand each of the three long-life deities. They were to be cast in copper, then gilded using gold leaf. Normally for this kind of commission all the craftsmen would gather in Lhasa, but on this occasion all the master craftsmen from Lhasa and Shigatse came to Tsetang, the region where I lived. They all stayed at the house of a master who was famous in our region and their expenses were paid for by the government. Although it was a large house, it was packed, as there were about one hundred and sixty of us working there. I did not stay in the house, since I could go back to my own home in the evenings to eat my meals and sleep.

Each of us was assigned one of the three deities, and my job was to

METAL WORKERS' BOWL, DHARAMSALA, INDIA

work on the statues of Namgya Ma. Since I was not yet fully trained, I was required to do only the embossing; the other stages were done by craftsmen who specialized in those particular processes. All the artisans of different trades would sit together, so I sat with the other craftsmen who were doing embossing. During the day, tea and *chang* (a Tibetan beer) were served to us while we worked. It was a relaxed and friendly atmosphere—we would talk and laugh and sometimes have picnics, and on occasion there would be drinking.

This was a very happy time for me and I felt confident that I would excel in my task. The painstaking and detailed work of embossing is the most important stage in the creation of a statue, as it brings out all the fine features of the deity. I was only nineteen at the time, and when I showed my work to my master and the others they were very pleased and impressed because I was so young. I was ordered to take the statue I had embossed and present it to each of the other one hundred and sixty craftsmen in turn and say, "This embossing has been done by me." Since it was an order, I had to do it. But I knew well what a good statue should look like and the qualities of fine embossing, so I really had no qualms. I felt I had done my part as well as it could be done. In all, I embossed about fifteen statues, each one taking about twenty-five days. Completing all three thousand took us about two years. These statues are now in the Norbulingka Palace in Lhasa.

Before beginning the construction of a statue, it is essential to perform a prayer ritual, or *puja*. If possible, this should be done at the beginning of the day, month, and year, with astrological calculations to determine the timing. First, one should make sure that the day, time, and position of the stars in the sky are auspicious and that many other factors are in harmony. For example, the craftsman should not be a hereditary blacksmith, or a butcher, or any other occupation considered to be of low status in Tibetan society. The most favorable situation is one in which the artisan doing the work is a monk, or, if that is not possible, then a layman who has taken the five basic vows—not to kill, steal, engage in sexual misconduct, drink liquor, or lie.

The artisan should cultivate the attitude of a *bodhisattva*, imagining that he is an embodiment of Vajrapani—the celestial bodhisattva who represents the concentrated power of all the Buddhas—regardless of what image he may be working on, and that his assistants are also heavenly beings. Everything associated with the task should be considered very sacred, even the clay or metal being worked on. Before starting work he should take refuge in the Buddha, *dharma* (the Buddhist teachings), and *sangha* (religious community). He should think of the image as being made for the benefit of all sentient beings. He should meditate and recite the mantra of the particular deity being fashioned. He must also seek the permission of the spirit of the earth before using her substance to create the deity, asking her to allow him to create the statue for the welfare of all beings.

After a statue is completed, the monks put written prayers and other sacred objects inside it and cover it with brocade. Then they gather all the statues together and sit for days performing a ritual of purification and blessing. It is recommended that viewers keep their eyes open when looking at a statue or thangka in order to receive the spiritual qualities inherent in it. Even if a viewer does not have a particularly reverent attitude, if his eyes see the image, he will receive the blessing of the deity's qualities.

After my two years of study with my third teacher, Dhembun Chola Eunghe, I began to work with him on a commission for twenty-one statues of Tara. When the statues were finished, it was easy to see that my work was just about as good as my teacher's. Having reached this level of ability, and thanks to the kindness and skill of my masters, I now felt confident that I could make any kind of statue. However, I was only able to work with my teacher for two years because the Chinese army came and occupied Tibet. It was as if day suddenly turned into night. At the time, the existing master craftsmen were quite aged and ready to retire, but

Metal Dragon on a Monastery Roof, Lachung Monastery, Sikkim

before they did so they were required by the government to select renowned craftsmen as their replacements. They had recommended Dorje Tsering and myself for the position, but because of the invasion this never came to pass.

Now my craft is at an end, as there are only three elderly masters surviving both inside and outside Tibet, of whom I am the youngest. There are other craftsmen doing this work, but it is not authentic, because it is not done according to tradition and the scriptures. I am trying to record my experiences, but since I only studied writing for six months as a child, you can imagine how slowly I write.

[THE GIFT OF GOOD WORK]
CHOE PHUNTSOK

My interest in building and repairing monasteries goes back as far as I can remember. As a child, it was my job to help with the goatherding, and whenever I took the goats up into the hills, I would let them feed in the pasture while I sat on a rock and constructed miniature monasteries and other buildings with small stones and pebbles. Some people from my village came to visit me recently, and I was astonished to hear that these structures are still standing! Even at this young age, I already had a great liking for carpentry and woodwork. When I took the goats to pasture I often used to cut a branch with my goatherd's knife and carve it into the shape of a butter bowl or a musical instrument. I still have the scars on my hands from the cuts I gave myself in my clumsy efforts all those years ago!

At fifteen I was helping my family transport grain on our yaks, traveling quite long distances to trade grain for salt and then the salt for rice, which we later traded at home for other goods. But my only desire was to do woodworking; so when I was twenty-two I began to study with my uncle, a famous carpenter. I lived at his house for a year and learned to make all kinds of things. I started with the specially designed boxes that we use to carry goods on horseback. Then I learned to make a musical instrument called a *damyang*, which is something like a guitar. I also made butter churns, small tables, water barrels, and drums. I learned very quickly, as I was bright and the skills came naturally to me. I was happy to be doing what I most wanted to do, and my uncle was happy to teach me, even though he had sons of his own.

My parents, however, were not pleased—they would have preferred me to put my whole heart into farming. I was the eldest of a family of eleven, and my parents insisted that as the eldest son I must help look after our family affairs. As a semi-nomadic family we had quite a bit of land but we still had to pay the government tax, so there was lots of work to do: looking after the yaks and other animals, working in the fields, and raising the goods we needed to sell in order to pay the tax. I was also expected to study, although I had little time for it.

Another reason for my parents' displeasure was that, in Tibetan society, carpentry and woodworking were not viewed as suitable occupations for people from families of high status. These trades were usually done by people from a lower level of society who had no other means of making a living, although a skilled woodcarver could often earn more than enough to meet his daily needs. In fact, as an independent craftsman having mastered the skills of woodcarving and monastery construction, I received very generous compensation and was treated very well.

After studying with my uncle for a year, I began to receive requests from different monasteries to do repairs and before long I was called to

Sakya to assist in the construction of the main temple of the Lama Sakyapa. It was there that I learned how to construct and carve a monastery in its entirety. These skills were passed on to me by a famous master carver named Dechen, who had been brought to Sakya from Lhasa to oversee the construction of the temple.

I studied with Dechen for three years, learning masonry, traditional engineering, geometrical drawing, and design, all under his expert guidance. I shall always feel indebted to my master for helping me learn my craft. He had nearly five hundred people working under him—masons, woodcarvers, carpenters, and laborers—but he gave me special attention because I was bright and took immense care with everything he asked me to do, so he could see that I was sincere in my desire to learn. It was customary for students and workers to offer gifts to their teachers, usually in the form of money or alcohol. But Dechen drank only tea and I knew the best offering I could give him was to do the finest work possible on whatever I was assigned to do; this was what pleased him most.

From the foundations to the roof of the monastery, my teacher guided my instruction and I was able to learn all the skills I needed. Wherever there was something important to be done, I was given the opportunity to assist in the work. I was always anxious to know what new thing I was going to learn the next day: how deep the foundations should be, what kind of stones should be used for them, where the pillars should stand, how to carve the different types of designs at the top of each structure. These were the things that concerned me, not how much I was getting paid or whether the job would come in on time.

My master decided that, since I was doing such good work and taking on a lot of responsibility, I should be given the title of *uchung*, which means something like "junior master "or "teacher." He went to see the man responsible for the construction of the monastery, a wealthy businessman from the Lhasa aristocracy whose name was Pondesang, and asked him if he would agree. I had other ideas, however. I told Pondesang that if my master felt like giving me an uchung's salary, I had no objections; I pledged to work to the standard of an uchung, but I did not want the social status that went with the position. I knew that, given the special relationship I had with Dechen, the many other uchungs from Lhasa who were working at the monastery would not be pleased if I took this title. Pondesang's response was that since I was a sincere and gifted worker, I had earned this privilege, and so I was given the salary of an uchung but not the title or status, just as I had requested.

By doing this I not only avoided problems for myself and my master, but at the same time was able to improve the overall quality of the work done in the monastery, which I knew I could only do as an ordinary worker. If I had taken the title of uchung while continuing to produce the high-quality work that I was known for, and then demanded work of a similar standard from the other craftsmen, they would simply have said, "You're an uchung, and it's your duty to do superior work!" However, as a normal worker, when I received commendations for the quality of my work I could say to the other uchungs, "My status is inferior to yours, but I am producing better work. So why can't you improve your skills and show the others how to do better, too?" In this way I was able to influence the general standard of work there.

Although with private commissions it was customary for offerings to be made to the master and his workers, the construction at Sakya was a government project, so the uchungs received no benefits other than their salary. During this three-year project I did not leave the construction site, since my main concern was to acquire all the skills from my master. In any case, I never had money to spend. There were official leave times, however, and during these periods my master, Dechen, would go and work on the Phunsok Potang—the private palace of the Lama Sakyapa. I was among fifteen skilled craftsmen working there under the master, and as well as our daily needs we were given many gifts of butter, meat, clothes, and money. Dechen was presented with gifts of great value, such as rich brocades, precious stones, *dzi*, and gold. The construction of this palace also took three years.

After the monastery and the palace were completed, Dechen returned to Lhasa. Before he left, he announced that he was very pleased with me, and that thanks to me his great burden of responsibility had been considerably lessened. I was told that my apprenticeship was complete and I was now ready to totally supervise the construction of a monastery. I returned to Tsang, where I constructed three new subsidiary monasteries to the great Namring Monastery, which took about four years. After that I went to Shigatse to work on the Panchen Lama's palace. I expected to be there for three years, but after two I was recalled to Namring to build a palace for the Panchen Lama and a congregation hall for the *geshes* (monks with high scholastic degrees). I completed both in two years.

I continued on in my profession, building small monasteries and temples as well as large private houses for wealthy families. There were few skilled craftsmen available, which meant I was very much in demand. Often a monastery and several families wanting new houses would call me at the same time, so unfortunately it was impossible for me to respond to every request. Because of the need, people appreciated me and treated me well. I would arrive on horseback at the main gates of whichever monastery had invited me, and even before I entered the monastery grounds a big picnic would be given to welcome me, often lasting the whole day. I would be given a whole new set of clothes and the monks would say special prayers for the successful completion of the monastery. At different stages of my work, I was offered large gifts, such as horses or yaks. Of course, these offerings were made only for private building projects. For government jobs, they would never stoop so low as to receive a master craftsman in this way!

My happiest times were during the period I worked on the palace of the Panchen Lama in Shigatse, which was a very auspicious undertaking.

By then I could work on my own. I had acquired almost all the skills of my craft and was able to handle almost every aspect of the work, thanks to the kindness of my own master, Dechen, who taught me everything I needed to know.

APPRENTICE AND TEACHER, SERA MONASTERY, TIBET

SHAKYAMUNI BUDDHA AND BUTTER SCULPTURES, SAMTEN CHOLING MONASTERY, GHOOM, INDIA

THE SHRINE HALL AND THE CARETAKER

GEKOE LOBSANG SAMDUP

For six years I was a caretaker, or *chabdri,* at Ganden Monastery and was responsible for the care of the main prayer hall and the shrine of the protector deity Palden Lhamo. Under me there were fourteen *dob-dobs,* or working monks, whose tasks included the upkeep of altars, water-offering bowls, and gardens, the playing of ceremonial instruments, and the performance of various offerings.

The position of chabdri is of great importance and responsibility; all the property of the monastery is in his hands. At Ganden Monastery this involved responsibility for seventy-three statues of Buddha, all of great age and value, as they came from India at the time of the Buddha himself. There were an equal number of shrines, as well as many gold and silver bowls and lamps. There were relics, including some belongings of the great saint Tsong Khapa, such as the cups from which he drank his tea and his mattress. There were also statues of deities, some of which were considered miraculous. One of these statues looks as if it were reaching out. It is believed that when Tsong Khapa was arriving at the monastery and the people gathered to receive him, the statue also stood up and said "I." It still looks as if it were preparing to meet Tsong Khapa.

I had many unusual experiences as the caretaker. Once, as I was passing through the front entrance, upon returning to the monastery's main prayer hall after having done some work elsewhere, I came upon some thieves hiding on the balcony of the prayer hall. Any other person probably would have been attacked, since it was the middle of the night. We later learned that the thieves had been planning to beat anyone who came in and they were armed with stones and other weapons. But they didn't dare touch me because I was well known for my anger. As soon as I saw them I banged on the door and some monks rushed in with lamps, and the three thieves ran away.

Another evening also comes to mind. There is a character in Tibetan monastic legends known as the *Geshe* with Horns and Donkey Ears. It is said that once there was a renowned geshe who was very competitive and jealous. All geshes must demonstrate their knowledge in monastic debate, and this geshe lost one particular debate. When he died, he took rebirth as a being with horns and a donkey's head. In the dead of night this figure appears in the monastery, wearing a monk's robe. If a monk meets him, he has to try to defeat the geshe in debate. If the monk is successful, the Geshe with Horns and Donkey Ears will run away, but if the monk is defeated, then it is said that either he will die or some disaster will happen to him. It was even believed that such a monk could become like the geshe, acquiring horns and donkey's ears. Most monks took this story very seriously.

Since my duty as caretaker involved the overall supervision of the main prayer halls, it was often quite late when I closed up the halls for the day. One evening, when I was about to close, I saw a monk in his robes, with his head lowered. It occurred to me that perhaps this monk was frightened of me. I went up to him only to discover that it was the Geshe with Horns and Donkey Ears. I was so scared that I fled from the room, banging the door behind me, and ran up the stairs. The monks upstairs heard all this and thought I was coming to discipline them, so they, in turn, became frightened. After some time, accompanied by some of my students, I returned to the main prayer hall. The Geshe with Horns and Donkey Ears was nowhere to be seen.

MONK LEAVING THE MAIN SHRINE HALL, THIKSE MONASTERY, LADAKH, INDIA

DANCE MASKS SITTING ON A SHRINE, TRANDRUK MONASTERY, TIBET

THE CALLIGRAPHER

GELONG LOBSANG DHONDEN

When I was thirteen, an official order came to my village announcing that fifty young children from well-to-do families were needed to work as servants or attendants for the Thirteenth Dalai Lama. As one of these fifty, I was taken to the summer residence of His Holiness in Lhasa, the Norbulingka. From this group the Dalai Lama personally selected seven boys. We were not asked any questions but were merely taken to a garden, where His Holiness observed us from a window. As we stood there with our hands in the position of prayer, I did not feel nervous but only prayed that I would have the chance to serve His Holiness, the emanation of the Buddha of Compassion. An aide had a list of all our names and recorded the Dalai Lama's choices. Those selected were made to stand separately and were told to come back the next day to begin the training. I was proud and excited to be one of the seven just as any Tibetan would be, given the opportunity to serve His Holiness. They called us *etuk*, meaning "selected children."

The following day we returned and were taken to our residence, which was a small house beside one of the palace kitchens. His Holiness had several secretaries, and one of them was assigned to training us. By then we were fourteen in number—seven from our region and seven from Gyantse. We studied for three years, during which time we trained in two types of calligraphy. The first is known as private handwriting and is used for unofficial writing, and the second is official handwriting for documents. After our studies we were tested and assigned work based on our performance. A boy from Gyantse and myself came in first in the class and were given a prize of some money, although my real reward was being assigned the task of copying letters written by His Holiness.

We were taught to use a board—sometimes thick and sometimes thin—on which we applied a layer of oil and then dusted very evenly with a fine white chalk powder. Once the document was written on the dusted board with an inkless bamboo pen, it was taken back to the Dalai Lama to be checked and corrected, then returned to my teacher for the final document to be created with ink on paper. Such a board was very useful, as it could be used again and again, and corrections could easily be made.

The office that I worked for was the Nangma Kang; today this is the Private Office of His Holiness the Dalai Lama. Officially there were four secretaries who assisted the Thirteenth Dalai Lama with his letters and communications. My teacher was one of these officials; after receiving the text of what His Holiness wanted written, he wrote it in a beautiful script called Tsomaque. At the age of fourteen, along with the other students, I was given a test. I received a very high score, and my teachers decided that I should continue my learning as an apprentice; I was to learn by doing. My first work concerned documents that recorded the donations to His Holiness. These particular offerings were made when there was a death in a family. My task was to prepare the official receipts and letters to these families and donors. In addition to learning the art of writing, we also worked at the Norbulingka doing other chores, such as planting flowers in the many gardens or caring for the Dalai Lama's dogs.

His Holiness was very fond of his dogs. One day my mother came from our village to see me, but when I asked for permission to visit with her, the Dalai Lama refused to grant my request. This happened during the Monlam prayer festival, when many monks took their religious vows. Since this ceremony required the entire day, I slipped out to search for my mother in Lhasa. Not long after this, on a very sunny and hot day, His

Holiness showed me one of his dogs and asked me why I had been so cruel and wicked as to leave it sitting in the sun. I told him that I had put the dog in the shade, but His Holiness took me by the hair and dragged me behind a shrine where some canes were kept, and gave me such a beating that I was bleeding when he was finished. What worried me most was that from then on I was forbidden to care for his dogs, and this meant that His Holiness was very annoyed with me. However, a short time later, he gave me some very fine clothes, made especially for me, and asked me not to go roaming around in the future. I realized then that I had received this beating not because of the dog, but for sneaking out against his wishes; it was through his supernatural powers that I was discovered. I had in fact placed the dog in a shaded area where His Holiness usually sat, but he must have moved the animal to a sunny place in order to find fault with me. Tibetans believe that beatings from teachers are helpful, and I feel that my good health and long life come from the small "blessing" beatings that I received from His Holiness the Thirteenth Dalai Lama.

As I progressed in my training as a calligrapher I learned a more refined form of official writing. This more elaborate form is done with bold or thick strokes; it is said that the vertical strokes should be like a strong man standing erect with shoulders firm. The capping of certain letters must be strong and distinctive, and the letters and words should appear as if they are raised up from the page.

We made our pens out of bamboo that came from a region near the border with China called Dartsedo. One particular village produced very good quality bamboo, from which they made the baskets that were used to pack the brick tea that came to Tibet. This village and its neighbors were required to provide the government with bamboo as a form of tax. The very best reed for pens came from a special kind of bamboo that was also used to make the struts of a red Chinese umbrella used in Tibet. This type of bamboo had three nodes close together, and the writing point would be made just below these nodes. Both students and government officials had to provide their own pens, and they often carried them about tucked into their long and sometimes elaborate hairstyles.

The inks that we used were of the best quality. This meant that if you were writing down dictation—for intance, if His Holiness were dictating a letter to the prime minister—one dip of ink would last a long time and no words would be lost. This ink was made from the bark of a pine tree from Rongpo and Takpo. The bark would be burned to produce a sooty residue, which was then combined with the burnt remains of a black or dark variety of barley. Sometimes a tree resin was mixed in, though not for the best inks, as this caused the ink to decompose. The highest-quality inks had a glossy and slightly oily appearance, which was due to the addition of an extract taken from the boiled *sukba* plant.

We used gold ink or paint to write the many glorifying titles that are given to the Dalai Lama, as His Holiness was never referred to by name. It was made by experts, usually thangka painters, since it was difficult to prepare. When writing any letter or document we would leave a space where His Holiness would write the date in his own handwriting. Then His Holiness would use one of his many seals to authorize the letter.

DEBATING LESSONS, NAMGYAL MONASTERY, DHARAMSALA, INDIA

DEBATING WITH THE ENLIGHTENED

LATI RINPOCHE

Debating is a form of meditation that has an aspect of developing or honing analysis, and also what is called contemplative or single-pointed meditation, which involves experiencing the insight that is conviction. In debating you yourself investigate and realize things. You see for yourself whether the path you are following leads to enlightenment. You can realize the nature of your own mistakes to a degree you could not attain simply by listening. Debating benefits your meditation and sharpens your understanding of wisdom.

While one can sit while debating, monks stand and take up certain positions. Each of these poses is significant and has a symbolic meaning. For example, by hitting one hand on the palm of the other, the debater should feel the destruction of the grasping self and the expulsion of the bad. If one hand is brought up and then the palm turned down to face the ground, this symbolizes the closing of the door to unfortunate states of rebirth or to bad migrations. When the other hand comes up and hits this hand, the debater liberates the beings from bad rebirth.

In 1959, when His Holiness the Dalai Lama took his geshe examination, I was privileged to be one of the few monks chosen to put questions to His Holiness in a debate. As we were to debate with one more learned than ourselves, our teachers naturally made sure that we were each well prepared. It is common for a monk to become totally confused by the responses of a more experienced debater. Nevertheless, after leaving the debating courtyard and returning to his room, opening the texts, and taking the time to think the matter through, the monk inevitably finds that he has learned immeasurably from the encounter. But to debate with His Holiness is to face even more than this. It is a very great responsibility.

All the monks from the three monastic universities—Sera, Drepung, and Ganden—were there; also attending were all the monks from the two tantric universities—Gyutho and Gyume. There were thousands in all. About one hundred monks were selected to debate with His Holiness. Some were to put forward questions in the morning, and others, including myself, in the afternoon. Friends of mine who were selected were famous debaters from the Upper and Lower Tantric colleges, since they were the most advanced and most experienced.

The time came and, although I had been taught over the years to debate well, I had great difficulty putting forward questions and debating with His Holiness. There were photographs taken of me and of others debating with His Holiness, but these photographs do not tell the truth. It felt as if I were asking His Holiness for the correct answer, rather than debating with him, which would have involved challenging him. Partly this was because His Holiness seemed then, as now, to have all the answers at his fingertips.

THE DALAI LAMA RECEIVING A LONG-LIFE BLESSING, NAMGYAL MONASTERY, DHARAMSALA, INDIA

FUTURES FORETOLD

Gekoe Lobsang Samdup

One time the Thirteenth Dalai Lama paid a visit to Ganden Monastery to oversee the renovations that he had ordered and to make a special prayer offering. I was nine years old then, and on that day five other young monks and I were playing with a pile of sticks—pretending that the sticks were a king, a minister, a thief, and various other characters. Suddenly, the eldest in our group said, "Stop, stop! His Holiness is coming." The Dalai Lama came up to us and asked our names. He asked one of my playmates the name of the oldest among us, and my friend answered "Lobsang Norbu" and pointed him out to His Holiness. "Don't call him Lobsang Norbu; call him Lama Sherla," His Holiness said, and he gave Lobsang an envelope wrapped in a white scarf. We didn't know it then but Lobsang was to go on to study for many years, receive his geshe degree, and become a renowned lama. His Holiness gave the rest of us some small sweets and told us that there would be a special offering the next day to which we should all come and share in the especially delicious porridge that would be served.

On the following day, we all received the porridge. We sat in the same place as the day before and once again His Holiness passed by, coming over to ask each of us what prayers we knew. When it came to my turn, I said that my father, who was a tantric yogi, taught me the Tara mantra. Then His Holiness asked what we had each received in our porridge. Lama Sherla said that he had found a raisin in his porridge, another boy discovered only one nut, and another friend had found just one piece of meat. When my turn came I said that I had found two pieces of meat, three raisins, and quite a lot of other dried fruit. His Holiness clapped his hand on my head and said that I was the luckiest of all our group. This has turned out to be true, because all those friends have since died, whereas I have lived long enough to serve the Fourteenth Dalai Lama.

DISGUISED IN THE MARKET

Sonam Dikyi

The Thirteenth Dalai Lama had a reputation for being very tough. His position was equivalent to king of Tibet, and it sometimes seemed as if he didn't enjoy this status. At times he would put on laymen's clothes—a dull red *chuba*, a hat, and a walking stick—and go into Lhasa to roam around where no one recognized him. Nowadays everyone is familiar with images of the Fourteenth Dalai Lama, but in the old days the Dalai Lamas were always in the palace, so no one really knew what they looked like. The Thirteenth Dalai Lama wandered around town, checking the prices that people were charging for various goods. If he thought they were higher than poor people could afford, when he got back to the palace he would tell the ministers responsible for such things that prices were too high.

He was strict about everything. For example, if one of the secretaries made a spelling mistake in an official letter or left something out, he would scold the person right there in front of everyone. He was very precise about things—spiritual practice, Buddhist doctrine, whatever it happened to be. It was he who established the dress code to differentiate aristocrats and government officials from lower-ranking individuals. Some of the merchants had considerable wealth and power and could afford many more servants than were usually found in the households of aristocrats and officials. The Dalai Lama insisted that dress should be based on rank, not on what you could buy, and so only officials working for the Tibetan government were allowed to wear pearls as jewelry or dress ornaments; the merchants could wear turquoise and things like that.

[POWA AND THE DEAD]
RINCHEN KHANDO CHOEGYAL

There was a sacred place near Degun where monks assembled once every twelve years. I was taken to this place while on a pilgrimage around U-Tsang to Lhasa and the surrounding areas. I remember how people sat on the rocks to receive the teachings from Degun Rinpoche. Though we were far away and could never hear those teachings, our faith was such that we deeply believed that if we were there, at such a time, then all our sins would be cleared away. It was also believed that there the teachings of consciousness transference known as *powa* were so powerful that, if you heard them in your lifetime, you would have no need at death. In fact, some of those who attended would bring with them the bodies of those who had recently died and lay their corpses on the rocks facing the lama. I was very frightened when I saw the dead. I can still feel the fear now as I think of it. Even then, though, part of me knew that the occasion was so very precious that people were right to take every possible advantage of the circumstance.

The occasion was both festive and solemn. People would bring many items for sale. While all the children like myself ran around and played, those who fully realized the importance of what was taking place were very serious, indeed, were in a state of meditation. It was a very special time.

FUNERAL PROCESSION PROCEEDING TO THE CREMATION SITE, LEH, LADAKH

PILGRIMS ON A HILLSIDE AFTER RECEIVING A BLESSING FROM A LARGE THANGKA, TASHILHUNPO MONASTERY, TIBET

AN EXCHANGE

Sonam Tsering

I was a trader for my master's monastery and I traveled regularly between Lhasa and Kalimpong. My job was to buy rice and cloth from India in exchange for salt and wool from Tibet. The best season for this journey was the winter because people all along the route would collect food for our animals; whereas in the summer, when everyone was up in the mountains with their own animals, we had to stop daily around midday just to let our mules and horses graze. Occasionally I made this trip alone, but usually we'd travel by caravan, with some distance between each group. Even though the route was difficult I never had any trouble. One time though, while journeying on an easier route from Tashilhunpo Monastery in Shigatse, I and another trader ran into difficulties.

This route winds along the shores of a sacred lake called Yamdrok Tso. At one point the land reaches out into the lake like the fingers of a hand. Travelers must make their way around each finger, unable to see what lies on the other side. On this occasion, as we rounded one such ridge, a group of bandits who had hidden behind some rocks began shooting at us. We took cover a couple of hundred meters away and shot back. While some of the bandits kept shooting, others tried to make off with our animals and goods. I had a single-shot rifle and fired a total of about fifteen to twenty shots. I killed two of the bandits and the remaining four ran away. We kept the rifles of the dead bandits, threw their bodies in the lake, and continued on, without any loss of goods or mules, and without having suffered any real harm ourselves, although I was grazed just below my armpit by one of the bandit's bullets.

We kept this fight a secret; it would have been dangerous to speak of it openly because the head of the local government would be sure to hear. If this official trusted us, then, of course, everything would be all right; but if he didn't, then we'd have to spend two or three days answering questions and trying to explain, which could have led to even more problems. We told my master and his household what had happened since they would have wondered how we had come by the new guns, and the lama was full of praise for how we'd handled the situation.

ROCKY PLAIN AND MOUNTAINSIDE, LHOKHA DISTRICT, TIBET

ENCOUNTER WITH A YETI

TSANGPA GYACHEN

In the summer I often went out hunting for two or three days, taking a tent and a yak to carry my supplies. I would usually hunt wild goat and antelope for meat and skins, using an old musket and handmade musket balls. All hunters and nomads had to be very careful of wild yaks since they were known to attack humans sometimes. The wild yak is huge—its head and horns can measure as much as five feet across and its tongue is so rough that it will take off not only skin but flesh as well. The yak licks until it sees blood, which is why they say that you should wear red underneath your clothing—if the yak attacks, it will stop when it gets to the red clothes.

The animals that gave us the most trouble were wolves. They could be a real problem because they killed sheep, goats, and horses, and even our yaks. In the autumn the wolves would give birth, and then they would be constantly killing sheep and goats to feed their cubs. The worst thing was that they would kill the animals and then just take the head. They trained their cubs by rolling the heads down steep slopes so the cubs would run after them—this was how they learned to hunt. Sometimes we would burn cow dung at night, and the fires might keep them away, but there was really very little we could do to protect our herds. Generally we didn't have much to fear from wild animals and I wasn't concerned for my life when I went hunting, but sometimes strange things happen.

One day, I was running after an antelope in a very narrow valley with a stream flowing through it. I had gone deep into the valley tracking this antelope and by the time I reached the valley's end I had lost the animal's tracks. There was no way I could climb up the rocky slopes because they were too steep, so I jumped over the stream and began to head back. I didn't see the yeti at first, but it must have been close to me when I jumped, because it took fright and ran away. He was big, like a yak running on all fours. His hair was long and reddish brown on the outside and black closer to the body, but his face was clean like a human's. There are two types of yeti: one type eats human beings and the other eats animals. The yeti that eats animals has a lot of hair on its face, but the one that eats people has a long hairless face, and very big ears. The one I met must have been the human-eating kind, since he had a smooth face.

The yeti ran some distance away, then sat down on a boulder and stared at me. I stared back. I thought about shooting him, but he hadn't tried to harm me, and anyway, old people say that killing a yeti is a very great sin. The yeti was trying to hide by making himself look smaller. Because of this, I felt he would not attack me and, although I was quite afraid, I didn't look back as I quickly walked back down the valley. I didn't realize that the yeti had started to follow me until suddenly he appeared just three feet away. I was on a very steep rock face and had no time to fire my musket, so I pulled out my knife and advanced toward him. The yeti, seeing the knife, thought the better of attacking me and ran off. That was the last I saw of him.

SKIN BOAT, SHORE OF YAMDROK TSO, TIBET

SKIN BOATS

TSERING DOLKAR YUTHOK

The boat often used in Tibet is called a *cowa; co* means leather. It's very tippy and in a strong wind is really very dangerous. I would always be seasick in a cowa when we went downriver, unless we traveled with two boats tied together. In a storm, if the boatmen have enough time, they try to take their cowa nearer to the shore, but they often get caught unawares and boats have been known to tip over and the passengers to drown.

When the boatman has to go upriver he takes to the land and walks with the cowa on his back. He always has a sheep with him as a helper, to carry the food and the boatman's things. These sheep eat the same food as the boatman—balls of tsampa—so they grow quite large and develop a coarser wool than other sheep. It was a common sight to see a group of boatmen, each walking with a boat over his head and each with a big, shaggy sheep following its master, the bell around its neck ringing with every step. Back on the water, the sheep just lies still in the boat, while the boatman either sings *nyemba,* boatman songs, or chants mantras as he rows and steers the cowa downriver.

HONORED AMONG THIEVES

NAGCHANG YESHE DORJE RINPOCHE: AS TOLD BY NAGPA KARMA LHUNDUP

Nagchang Yeshe Dorje would often speak of an incident that happened to him in the Chang Tang region of Tibet. This vast area of grasslands and endless plains is home to many notorious bandits. Yeshe Dorje was wandering alone through this region when he encountered a group of bandits who recognized him as a *nagpa*, a shaman employed to work spells and perform rituals. They escorted him to their hideout, saying that the chief's wife was having great difficulty in delivering her baby, and they wanted Yeshe Dorje to assist.

By making feast offerings, reciting mantras, and performing rituals and visualizations he empowered some butter and fed this to the bandit's wife. These practices went on throughout the day and well into the evening, and when there was still no sign of the baby emerging he began to worry. Finally, the bandit's wife gave birth. The baby was dead, but to the great relief of the bandits the chief's wife had survived. After this, they placed greater faith than ever in Yeshe Dorje. Bandits, like everyone in Tibet, had faith in any lama, but far more so in one who could demonstrate an ability to cure. So the bandits took him to a cave hidden in a crater, where they lived, and offered him many kinds of food and asked him to perform numerous ceremonies and long-life initiations.

After staying for some days he told them it was time for him to move on. The chief of the bandits gave Yeshe Dorje an official letter carrying his personal stamp and told him, "As you go, you will come across many other bandits. They all come under my jurisdiction. Each time they stop you, show them this letter and they will help you." So Yeshe Dorje continued on his way, encountering bandits every few days, staying with each band and conducting the religious rituals that were always asked of him.

Pilgrim Circumambulating Hermitage, Tashi Dorje Hermitage, Lake Namtso, Tibet

MOUNT KAILAS

ZASEP TULKU RINPOCHE

After I had been at Sera Monastery for one year, my grandfather said that it was very important for me to go to Mount Kailas. It was not easy to get permission for the journey. The abbot of Sera Je said, "No, the little *tulku* should be in the monastery studying philosophy." He was serious about this. He asked my grandfather, "Why are you going to Mount Kailas?" My grandfather replied, "Oh you know, circumambulating rocks and the mountain." My grandfather told me that this time the abbot wouldn't give his permission, but that he would try again. "You have to ask again and again," he said. "This is the way with traditions. You have to push and push. Maybe I will have to ask three times." Fortunately, the abbot agreed on my grandfather's second request, with the stipulation that he must bring me back within seven or eight months. I don't know whether grandfather knew or sensed the urgency for such a trip, but three or four months after our return the Chinese army invaded Tibet and many of the monasteries that my grandfather showed me on this pilgrimage were destroyed.

We stayed for two months at Mount Kailas, and it was a wonderful time for me. In the mornings, because I was a *tulku* (a spiritual teacher that takes successive rebirths for the benefit of beings), I had to memorize sacred texts as well as perform different rituals and spend a couple of hours in informal study. There was also the task of collecting the beautiful, different-colored sands, which were traditionally taken to all parts of Tibet and given to people to put on their fields as a blessing. We also went down to the huge lake to collect fish. This didn't involve actually catching the fish, but rather searching for ones that were already dead. These fish from the sacred Lake Manasaravor were said to be very good, especially for pregnant women, as they enabled them to have a swift labor. We would look all along the shoreline for those fish already dried by the ele-

ments, so that they could be brought back and distributed. These two tasks, collecting the sand and the dead fish, were a wonderful pastime.

Lake Manasaravor itself I found very exciting, partly because of the legends about it. I first recall these from my time at Sakya Monastery. In the protector puja rooms, as in other monasteries, there were stuffed animals—a cow, a horse, and a sheep. I was told that all these stuffed animals were from Lake Manasaravor. The fact that they *all* had very curly sheep's wool—one does not usually see curly haired horses or cows—seemed good evidence for people's beliefs that all these animals came from out of the lake. The legend is that there are lake sheep, lake horses, and lake oxen. The sheep live under the water, so the story goes, and dive into the lake and sleep there, coming out every now and then to eat some grass before diving back in. I was very impressed by this legend, and throughout our stay at Kailas I went looking for these animals. Every now and then I would see a rock and would say to myself excitedly, "Ah, an ox!" I was attracted most of all by the idea of the sheep, though. Each time, during those months, when nomads came to Lake Manasaravor with their flocks, I would look carefully at the animals, wondering whether these were lake sheep and whether they were on their way back to the lake.

The day came when my grandfather said we must begin our return journey, but I didn't want to leave. He sat me on the horse, but I kicked my feet and shouted, "I'm not going!" I cried and cried. I just felt that I wanted to live there, that I didn't want to go back east or anywhere else, that I didn't care; all I wanted to do was to stay there. There is nothing at Mount Kailas, of course—it is utterly barren—but I so loved the lake and the mountains. This attachment that I felt was an extraordinary experience.

YAKS GRAZING, SOUTHERN BASE OF THE NYENCHEN TANGLHA, TIBET

SALT CARAVAN

TSEWANG TASHI

Like many other Tibetans, I grew up in a family of nomads who made their living by raising animals. Out of our income we made offerings to the deities, gave alms to the poor, and paid taxes. We owned about five hundred yaks (male) and *dri* (females), as well as sheep and goats. From the time I was eight or nine, I was expected to help take care of the animals. I can still see myself going up into the mountains early in the morning and coming back at night. In fact, we had so much livestock that it took quite a few family members to look after them all.

When I was fifteen, I began to go on trading trips with members of other families. Traveling in groups of about thirty people, we went north once a year on a very important journey—to collect salt. We carried guns for protection and since each of us took about twenty yaks to bring the salt back, we formed a large caravan of around six hundred yaks. Salt is very useful and everybody needed it, so the yaks that we took on this journey were not just our own. Those families that could not go to collect salt for some reason would lend their animals and ask others to get the salt for them. In exchange for this help, the salt collectors were given barley by the nomads who stayed at home. To reach the Golok region near Derge, it took at least twenty-five days on horseback, but longer in the spring, when there wasn't enough grass growing yet to feed the yaks properly.

We usually started our day's journey early in the morning and would ride until noon, after which we would let the animals graze for the rest of the day. In the evening, each family gathered its own animals and made a square pen, by sticking wooden poles into the ground and connecting them with ropes. Then we would tie the animals to the ropes all around the enclosure and pitch our yak-hair tent in the center of the square. On our return trip, the many bags of salt would be piled in the tent for safekeeping. About four or five families would gather together to create a common kitchen and prepare tea and meals, but there were never any women on these trips.

When the caravan was about two days' journey from a large saltwater lake, we would leave the animals behind to be cared for by one person from each family while the rest of us went ahead to get the salt. In the springtime, collecting salt was easier because it was found all along the shore. But in the summer, when the water level was higher, we had to dig for the salt, then painstakingly clean it, since the salt was now mixed with the sand at the water's edge.

The sandy salt would be scooped into a bag or blanket made out of yak hair, which was then put into the water, where someone stomped on it repeatedly. The water was so salty that the salt did not dissolve, but the sand and mud washed away. I remember clearly that this work was very painful because our feet were in the salty water so much that they developed sores. Usually, it took five days to collect all the salt we were going to take back. After the gathered salt had been spread out and dried in the sun, someone was sent to fetch the yaks. Once the animals were loaded with the bags of salt, we began our journey home.

This method of getting salt was really quite an easy one. We just went there, got the salt, and brought it home. In other parts of Tibet, more difficult methods were employed—such as using sheep to collect the salt.

NOMAD CAMP, BETWEEN GANDEN AND SAMYE MONASTERIES, TIBET

TO THE NOMAD CAMPS

JAMYANG SAKYA

In 1953 my husband, Sakya Rinpoche, was invited to eastern Tibet, and I joined him on the journey, eager to revisit the area where I grew up. We took a northern route, and, since there were few monasteries on the way, we often camped. The tent we used for our family had been made in Bhutan and was constructed of heavy, striped canvas and had a window. My husband's tent, which he used for religious ceremonies, was particularly beautiful and was made of gold canvas and decorated with Buddhist symbols and red and blue dragons. This special tent was set up wherever there were enough visitors to warrant it, and it was visible from a long way off.

There were many nomads scattered over this vast area and, though they lived in dispersed communities, news traveled fast—people quickly learned if a lama was coming, especially a Sakya lama. Each evening when we stopped to camp, hundreds of nomads from miles around would gather to see, and be blessed by, Sakya Rinpoche. Many came by horseback, while others rode yaks or walked. As more and more people arrived there would be many joyful reunions, with old friends hugging and kissing each other. The people were very affectionate and had a closeness I had not seen before.

My husband gave Buddhist teachings to the nomads and distributed blessing cords or relics. The nomads were extremely devout; they never asked for elaborate things such as initiations and so on, but would be content simply to be touched on the head by the lama, receiving the blessing of the Buddha, the bodhisattvas, and the Sakya lamas. They had so much faith and trust; they believed that a real Buddha was present. They expressed profound respect for all lamas and monks, not just for those from our school of Buddhism. They would crowd around Sakya

Rinpoche, and, though the monks would scold them and tell them to get back, I would always ask the monks to leave them be since it was their only chance to see Rinpoche.

When the nomads entered my husband's tent they would immediately prostrate themselves on the ground and ask my husband such questions as "How many years will we live?" My husband would say, "Oh, don't ask me. I don't know. I don't even know how long I'm going to live!" "Oh, yes, you do know!" they would reply, "Just tell us!" Sometimes Sakya Rinpoche would tell them to perform a puja or to recite certain daily prayers and then they would live for a certain number of years. At other times he would say that perhaps in a couple of years that person might face difficulties, but that later he or she would be fine. Years later, when we met the nomads again, they told us that it had happened exactly as Rinpoche had predicted. That was a demonstration for me of why faith is so very important. The nomads were the most devout people I have ever met.

There was nothing modern about the nomadic way of life. Daily life was slow-paced and no one ever hurried. People just sat, or lay down, and talked. People would speak openly and simply about whatever was in their hearts. The nomads would always bring butter, cheese, and yogurt for Rinpoche to eat. They thought that if he ate a little bit then their family would prosper or their animals would be blessed, so they would always insist that he take a little bite. Often people would ask Rinpoche for blessings on behalf of elderly relatives or sick animals, requesting blessings for them.

The best gift you could give the nomad women was a kind of makeup, though not the Western type. It was the red paper that was used as a wrapping for tea leaves. These beautiful women would lick the wrapper and dab the red color onto their cheeks, doing all this quite openly. It was wonderful to watch. They would wear or use anything that we gave them, whether it was tea leaf wrappers, beads, or glasses.

My abiding memory of that time is that even when the nomads had work or chores to do they would resolutely stay all night near the lama.

Although the women would claim that they were going back to their tents to sleep, I would still hear them outside our tent. They all wore lots of jewelry hanging around their necks or braided in their hair, so almost all night long, as they walked around our tent on *kora*, together with the sounds of whirring prayer wheels and mumbled prayers, I could hear the soft tinkling of their jewelry.

[AMBER]

KELSANG TASHI

One day, my sister and I were out tending the herds of yaks, goats, and sheep on the side of a mountain. We'd just finished eating our lunch when we happened to see an outcrop of yellow stone. The recent rain had washed it clean and it was a beautiful yellow color and it had a special smell. When I hit it with another stone, we noticed that it made a different and unusual sound. I had heard my parents talk of amber, but I didn't know if that was what we'd found. I was about ten years old at the time, and the main thing my sister and I knew was that the stone had a very good smell, which was why we decided to collect it. We dug and scraped with sharp rocks and managed to chip off pieces that looked like bits of wood. In the end we only got maybe four kilograms back to our tents; there was so much that if we'd wanted to carry all of it we'd have needed a horse.

Back at our camp we showed everyone what we had found and they said the stone was indeed amber and was very precious. Our parents told us to return to the same place the next day and get more, so I went back with a friend. It wasn't far away, perhaps seven kilometers, but when we got to the site, there was not a trace of amber, only stone like the rest of the mountain. We returned home and told everyone the amber had disappeared. My grandfather said that it was the property of the earth spirit and that the spirit had reclaimed it by turning the amber into ordinary stone. My parents told me that, in the future, if I found any beautiful or precious stones, I should leave them be because removing them would decrease the power of the earth. Mind you, they only told me this after I came back the second time, when we'd seen the amber was gone! As nomads, we soon traveled on, and I never came across the place again.

NOMAD WOMAN WEAVING, SUMED TIBETAN NOMAD CAMP, LADAKH, INDIA

NOMAD SHEPHERD, LAKE NAMTSO, TIBET

THE SLEEPER AWAKES

LOBSANG GYALTSO

One member of my father's household was always sleepy, from the time he was young to when he was eighteen. Being a few years younger, I had to help him take care of the yaks. Everyone knew that instead of tending to the animals he would fall asleep, so my father's family used to insist that whoever went with him should try to keep him awake. In Tibet people believe that in a deep sleep you're in danger from ghosts and spirits. We herded the yaks to the pasture and, as usual, he said to me, "You look after the animals while I take a little nap," and he lay down, face up, on the side of a small hill. I waited and, sure enough, he fell into a deep sleep. So I decided to teach him a lesson.

I looked around and came up with a plan. He had long hair—like many lay people in Tibet—so I tied his hair to his rope belt and the belt to a nearby tree. Then I tied his legs together and tied these to another tree. I spread his arms out to either side and put wet *dzo* dung in each palm. Then I made a kind of ball out of a special plant that has leaves that are dry and burn slowly, like incense. I lit this and put it on his nose, and then I hid in a tree with a lot of cover, some distance away. Slowly the fire and heat worked its way down. To begin with, he moved just a little. Then, as it really began to heat up, he started to grab at his face with his dung-filled hands until he'd completely covered himself in dung. Next he tried to get up, but his head and feet were tied to the trees. It took him a while to figure it out, but finally he freed his hair and then managed to untie his feet.

He looked around, rubbing some of the dung off his face with his chuba and snatching up all the stones he could find. He was very angry and rushed here and there trying to find me. I knew that if he did, those stones were meant for my head. He went to search on the other side of the hill, where the animals were grazing, and I jumped down from the tree and made a run for it. Some distance toward home, I stopped and looked back. He saw me and started yelling, "You did this, and I'm going to get you and. . . ." I continued running! When I got back, my family asked me why I'd returned so early. I said they'd find out soon enough and I told one of my sisters to go up the mountain. After a while she came back, and before she was even inside the house she was shouting that I had treated my relative very badly. At the same time she couldn't stop laughing. My family got together and talked about it. Afterwards everyone would laugh, then they'd scold me, and then they'd burst out laughing again.

The following day, this fellow was still very angry. But all the family members held a meeting with both of us present, and they told him that he should feel grateful to me because if a person falls into a deep sleep his spirit can be taken by a ghost or evil spirit. They said I'd done an excellent job of waking him up!

Nomad Butchering Sheep While His Son Digs a Hole for the Animal's Dung, Sumed Tibetan Nomad Camp, Ladakh, India

LIKE CURES LIKE

NORGYA THE NOMAD

Our herd of yaks once suffered a terrible disease and only a few animals survived. Before the illness hit we had about 250 yaks and around 2,700 sheep and goats. To help us restock our herd, the local monastery gave us two hundred yaks and *dri*. In return, our family provided the monastery with a set amount of butter from these dri, keeping for ourselves what remained. As well as the animals supplied by the monastery, we bought sixty to seventy animals with money we'd made transporting salt and barley.

I was ten years old when the sickness that killed our yaks arrived; we called the disease *yor.* The first sign of yor is that the animal loses its appetite and its stool becomes bloody. Then the animal starts acting a little crazy and, a few days later, it dies. To prevent the spread of yor we'd cut a certain vein in a sick animal's neck from which the blood flowed out like water from a tap. A small jug would be filled with the sick yak's blood; this blood was divided in half and fed to two healthy animals by pouring it down their throats through a yak horn. Soon these animals would also become a little sick and after two or three days they would be bled and this bad blood fed to more healthy animals. This treatment was then repeated throughout the herd. It is a very old practice and after being treated the yaks won't get yor. My father could have protected our herd from yor but that year he didn't do what was necessary.

Although the disease doesn't come every year, it can return after five, six, or even ten years. In preparation for this we'd take a white yak tail, dip it into the blood of a sick animal, and dry the bloody tail in the sun. Then we'd seal this tail in a copper pot, making sure the lid was put on really tight so that no air could get in. Whenever the disease returned, the tail was taken out, put into fresh blood, and the blood given to the animals as before.

Another far more dangerous disease for both yaks and humans is called *saduk.* With saduk an animal becomes lazy and stops eating grass. Its nose becomes dry and growths appear around its eyes. There is also a black swelling near the animal's spleen. To treat the animal, we would cut out this growth and remove blood from the spleen. We'd find a particular soft spot around this swelling with our fingers and with a long, sharp piece of bamboo we'd push hard and deep into his body and draw out some blood. Fire medicine—burning the tips of the animal's horns and hooves with a red-hot iron—could also be used as a treatment. If these treatments are carried out when the disease first appears, the yaks and dri may recover. Without treatment, the sick yaks begin to wander around, charging animals and people, becoming crazier and crazier until, after a day or two, they die.

This whole time was really dangerous for us and for the rest of the animals because if the smallest amount of a sick animal's blood got on one's skin, one's whole body would swell up. So if we had to work with these animals, we had to go to a yogi to receive a special mantra or prayer. When a person died of saduk we wouldn't give him a sky burial—feeding his body to the birds and animals—nor would we put his body in the river, which is our usual custom. Instead, the body had to be buried in the ground. A yogi would say a mantra over the body and sprinkle a mixture of black sand and white stones so that those who buried the body would be protected. If a person contracts saduk but doesn't die, then he will always be safe from the disease and, even years later, can tend to those sick with it.

WOMEN GATHERED TOGETHER TO MAKE DUMPLINGS, KALACHAKRA INITIATION, JISPA, LAHAUL, INDIA

A Nomad's New Year

Kayma Lhamo and Pema Thinley

Losar, or Tibetan New Year, is a time of purification. On the twenty-eighth and twenty-ninth days of the twelfth month of the Tibetan calendar, we nomads all clean our tents and make ceremonial statues from flour. First we mix barley flour, butter, and water to make a dough called *pak*, and then we touch parts of our bodies with this dough to remove any illnesses. With the same pak we make statues in the shape of humans. We collect the dirt and soot by cleaning the tent and hearth and use it to blacken the statues. The men of the camp then gather up all the statues and take them far away from the tents. While this is being done everyone prays that all the evil will be taken away with these statues. When carrying them away the men must not look back toward the tent. Once they are away from the camp the men make a fire and toss the statues on the flames along with the rest of the flour. Only the men may do this, not the women. Men from two or three families join together in this purification ceremony, and if one has a gun he shoots at the statues as they burn while the others use slings to hurl stones. After burning the statues each man returns to his tent where his wife asks, "What have you brought?" The man answers that he has brought gold—which, of course, he hasn't! At the door to the tent the woman offers a black stone and the man offers a white stone in return. He then throws away the black stone but keeps the white one to bring good luck for the coming year.

On the same day as cleaning the tent and destroying the statues, we make a special noodle soup called *thukpa* for dinner. Within this soup are small flour balls, inside of which we put many things, such as a piece of broken china, some sheep dung, a piece of wool, and so on, each of which has a special meaning. Everyone who is given a bowl of thukpa will get one of these little dumplings in his or her portion, and will open it to see what it has to tell. If you find sheep's dung inside, it means that you are very clever. If you find coal, it means you are cruel and have a black heart. If you find a piece of a broken, white porcelain bowl, it means your heart is pure. Finding a stone means long life. If you receive a piece of bone, it means that you are very high up, like a king. A dumpling with a ring in it means the person is cheap and doesn't want to spend his money. A dough ball containing a few strands taken from a rope used to tie up sheep and goats means you could become rich. If you get meat in your dumpling, it means you are really sinful! Along with the dumplings, there's also a little flour figure of a woman and child in the soup; this foretells the birth of a child. Only the house mother or father can put this figure on your plate—you can't go choosing it. When everyone sits down together to eat this soup there's always a lot of fun and laughter.

Hermits' Attendant in Cave Kitchen, Tashi Dorje Hermitage, Lake Namtso, Tibet

NINE BOWLS

GESHE TASHI NAMGYAL

Losar, Tibetan New Year, is a wonderful time. On the twenty-ninth day of the twelfth month, the New Year's ceremonies begin with a day of cleansing, or purging, the monastery. At midday we monks would begin to collect all of the old offerings, the ritual cakes and other food; in the evening, we would throw them away, thus "cleaning the slate" in preparation for the new year. After we had finished this task, a wonderful, thick soup was prepared, the most special soup of the year. Though I can only speak for that of my own community, each community had, no doubt, its own special variant of this soup. We would always work with nine ingredients. These would include meat, tsampa, and various types of wheat, but there always had to be nine ingredients. The soup was cooked in a most elaborate manner. Now, we had different sizes of bowls; for this particular soup, we used our smallest bowls because we were each required to consume nine bowls of soup. I am not sure whether I could separate the excitement I felt at the coming of this wonderful soup from that of the coming of the new year.

As a child, when I was still living at home, in preparation for Losar we also would clean the house, on the thirtieth. I remember getting up the following day, very early on the morning of the first day of the new year, at about one or two o'clock, and my mother would serve *chang*, a Tibetan beer, which we mixed with tsampa and cheese. This was the first of the day's special meals. After drinking this we always talked for a while before returning to bed.

At about seven or eight o'clock in the morning we would again rise, and my mother would make a special meal of meat dumplings accompanied by another wonderful soup. This, too, was always a joyous occasion. Afterwards important preparations for the day would begin. A sheep or goat would be taken, butchered, and the head cooked. For lunch we ate every last part of this boiled head, except for the bones, and it was quite a delicacy. Afterwards people would drink a lot of chang and gamble and dance. It is no wonder Losar is so warmly anticipated; celebrations often go on for over a week. Even very poor people celebrate, though maybe only for one day.

In the monasteries the celebrations spanned three days. The meals were quite similar to those of lay people but no alcohol would be consumed. In the very early morning we drank salt and butter tea, along with sweet rice. Afterwards we would gather in the large communal prayer hall and perform long sessions of prayers and make offerings. At midday we would have a meal of soup and bread, and later a sheep's or goat's head would be eaten.

For us, the most important quality of Losar was that, compared to the strict discipline we monks usually followed, these three days were very relaxed. While during the rest of the year debating represented one of the most crucial aspects of our lives, at Losar there was no debating or study of dialectics.

MONASTERY KITCHEN, TRANDRUK MONASTERY, TIBET

TEA AND PORRIDGE FOR 2,500

GEKOE LOBSANG SAMDUP

For one memorable year, I was the head of one of the large kitchens at Ganden Monastery, where we prepared food for as many as 2,500 monks. I had twelve monks working under my supervision, and when extra help was needed, we called for the *dob-dobs,* the monks who did most of the physical work within the monastery. Twice a day, using huge cauldrons and enormous kettles, we prepared tea, and once a day we cooked a porridge made of wheat. Since the monks ate a simple diet, this was actually quite an easy task. My main job was to make sure that the correct amounts of the various ingredients were used, and that they were properly cooked. You might not think so, but the right quantity of salt and butter is crucial when making Tibetan tea. Often there was a prayer ceremony in the morning, so we would begin to boil the water for the tea the night before. Since the kettle was a very large one, holding up to a thousand gallons, it was necessary to keep the fire going all night. Once the water was boiling, up to sixteen bricks of tea were added and mixed in with long ladles. While the monks stirred the tea they sang a prayer, "Ah—Ha—Ho—Ah—Hung," and this chant could be heard throughout the monastery grounds. So much tea was used by our monastery that local farmers would come to the kitchens and cart off the used tea to feed it to their animals and to spread it as fertilizer in their fields.

I remember the four large, six-foot-high tea churns, sunk deep into the ground of the kitchen floor, that would be filled with butter and salt. Into each churn would go twenty-five or thirty kilograms of butter, often supplied by the prayer ceremony's sponsor. The butter came in huge lumps packed in yak hide and it took a really strong monk to pick one up. During each tea time, hundreds of kilograms of butter were used. The churns were held down by a few dob-dobs, while others did the churning. At the start of churning, the strength of two dob-dobs was needed to

work the plunger, which made the sound "dang-chang, dang-chang." When the butter was mixed in with the tea, two or three monks would lift the churns by their attached ropes and pour the butter tea back into the kettle. This churning process had to be repeated ten times to make all the tea. Then I would come down from the fireplace and go off into a cool corner of the kitchen to taste the tea. I might do this tasting two or three times each morning, until the tea was just right.

When the tea was finally ready, a gong was sounded to call the dob-dob servers to the kitchen. They all came running with their serving pots, anxious to be first in line to get the tea and take it back to the thirsty congregation of monks! The servers were so excited and wild that monks with sticks stood around the kettle to beat and control them. When these servers were hit, it wasn't like beating human beings because they just didn't care. It was a matter of great pride for those dob-dobs to be the first back into the prayer hall with the delicious tea.

While the tea was being churned, a monk would make his round of the monastery with a gong to remind the other monks of a particular legend or story. In one story a deity's servant called Adzer milks a snow lion and puts the milk into the tea. In another, that same Adzer keeps the fires lit under our kettles with basketfuls of dung cakes. It was due to Adzer's power that the dung cakes burst into flames by themselves!

In addition to the twice-daily tea, we would occasionally make a special rich porridge of rice called *paksuma*. It looked like rice pudding, but was much thicker. As chief cook I was responsible for making sure that the right amounts of water and other ingredients were used—not an easy task, since the cauldron used to make this porridge was enormous. When I was a very young boy, this cauldron was brought in pieces over the Himalayas by a wealthy business family. These pieces were then reassembled with large iron bolts. We used these bolts that stuck out from the sides of the cauldron as a way of measuring the amount of water required for cooking. To clean the cauldron, I had to send several monks down inside to scrape its sides with shovels. It was so big that thirty to forty monks standing side by side were needed just to surround it. During the *geshe* examinations sixty *kels* (1,200 kilograms) of rice were used to prepare the large amounts of porridge needed to feed everyone at the gathering.

To make paksuma, butter was first melted in the cauldron and then drawn up the sides to harden, after which the water was poured into the pot up to the eleventh bolt. To make sure the quantity was accurate, a separate pot was used to mix the salt and water and then this mixture was poured into the cauldron. After I tasted the water to see if the amount of salt was correct, the rice would be added from four sides of the cauldron, while from two other points kitchen workers stirred with large wooden paddles.

I kept a close watch at this time, and when the cauldron became red hot at the bottom, I would give the signal that no more fuel be added to the fire. After hours of cooking, when the mixture finally rose to the fourteenth bolt, I knew that the water had boiled off and the porridge was ready. Another way I could tell was to put my ear to the side of the cauldron and listen to the sound of the cooking. If it sounded like "pick, pick, pick," then the porridge was going to be very good; but if I heard "bloop, bloop, bloop," I was about to be in a very embarrassing position.

In order to boil the water and cook the rice for this porridge, the fire would be started the day before at about five in the evening. By nine that same night I would call out that the fires should be pulled away and the cooked rice covered with sacks. Then we would go to sleep. In the early morning, a monk would come and say a prayer over the porridge. Twenty-five more buckets of melted butter would be added to the cooked porridge, along with three or four large basins of dates, pieces of fried yak meat, and some more salt. Sixty dob-dobs would come to help and mix the porridge with a large wooden paddle. The paddle had ten ropes attached at its middle, and at the end of each rope was a dob-dob ready to pull the paddle toward himself, while five others held on to the paddle itself. They moved all around the outside of the cauldron, with great bursts of back and forth movement, mixing the porridge from different sides, while the other monks added butter or just gave advice.

During the mixing more ingredients were added, such as raisins, almonds, and apricots. When the mixing was finished, the porridge was tamped down to make it level; if hit in one spot, the whole thing rolled and settled into place. Then the sponsor of the puja would be called to check the porridge, after which he would come to see me as the head cook. If he was pleased I was thanked and perhaps given a gift. This special porridge was usually made two or three times a month, but during the winter prayer festival called Gunchoe it was made every day for fourteen days in a row and required a great deal of work on our part.

Just as with serving the tea, when it came time to serve the porridge it was very dangerous and there was lots of pushing, shoving, and fighting. One hundred and fifty dob-dobs, from all the different monastery sections, would arrive with their serving buckets to see who would be the first to get the porridge from the kitchen back to his prayer hall. Shovels were used to load the porridge quickly into their buckets while forty to fifty other monks tried to keep order by using sticks to control this wild competition. Once outside the doors of their large prayer halls the servers would wait for the order to start. Then they would all rush in and start serving the food, first to one monk, then another and another, moving very quickly down the rows of monks. The servers used heavy metal ladles that had beautiful wooden handles with red pieces of cloth fastened to their tips for decoration. With one scoop and a slap, each monk's bowl was filled. Anyone who got in the dob-dobs' way was simply pushed aside. You might think that all this happened without order or discipline, but the monks with the sticks kept everyone in line. If a server received even ten hits with the sticks, he would not be angry. He just accepted it.

MONASTERY KITCHEN WORKER, THIKSE MONASTERY, LADAKH, INDIA

BLESSED FOOD BEING DISTRIBUTED TO THE CROWD, KALACHAKRA

INITIATION, JISPA, LAHAUL, INDIA

GENEROUS COUSIN

YESHI JIMPA

In Tibet there is a saying: "When beggars' children are naughty, their parents threaten to send them to work." We Tibetans always took care of beggars, I suppose because of our religious beliefs. Most beggars did not have too difficult a life; they would rarely be turned away empty-handed.

Once my cousin, who ran a store, became sick and asked my father to manage the shop for her. In the store there was a drawer full of money, to be handed out to any person who sought alms. On this particular day some beggars came into the store, and, as is customary, my father gave them some money. What he did not know, unfortunately, was that after accepting the money, the beggars were walking around the store and rejoining the line of those waiting for alms. My father failed to notice that the same faces kept appearing. Eventually the beggars swindled him out of all the money in the alms drawer.

My family also owned a store. It was one of five rooms in a building we owned, and the other four were our living quarters. The store sold all kinds of things, ranging from pots and pans to incense sticks and hats. The only thing we didn't sell was food. It was a small but well-kept store, with most of our goods kept outside under a tentlike roof, as is customary in Tibet. We had no chimney, so there was often a smell of burning wood inside, especially when my mother cooked in the other part of the house. The thick smoke spread into the store in great clouds, coating everything black and making it hard to keep the store clean for very long. I can still remember the smell of this store.

Running a store was a less complicated business there than in the West. There were no set hours; we could open and close whenever we felt like it. My parents often closed the shop when the weather was good and did what all Tibetans love to do—go on a picnic. There were many, many times we would go down to the river in Lhasa, just to sit and enjoy the weather and the nature around us. Our family led a simple life.

THE BEGGING CLASSES

TSERING DOLKAR YUTHOK

Although beggars came to Tibetan homes every day, there were two special days when large numbers would arrive at the homes of noble families. In our house this custom of offering tsampa to whoever should arrive on the fifteenth and the thirtieth day of each month started in the time of my grandfather. On these two days beggars would form two lines in our courtyard and an appointed leader would make their request. After receiving a portion of tsampa, each beggar would continue on his way.

Beggars in Tibet could be divided into different classes. The *regyabas* had the highest status in the begging community. They would assess the needs and problems of their community and call on the lower classes of beggars to take charge of particular tasks. The regyabas also had a role to perform in the wider community. They would collect the bodies of the unclaimed dead and deliver the corpses to the sky burial place or do whatever was required for each particular body. The rest of the time they engaged in their other part-time job, which was begging.

It was remarkable how the regyabas always knew when a special event was to happen at a family's home. Even though such occasions were private, they would always be there, waiting. They were only allowed to beg on certain occasions or at formal events, such as weddings, when a family achieves a higher status. They would arrive in the courtyard and shout, "We, the regyabas, are here," and tell us the number of people in their group and their demands for a certain amount of money. Families had no choice but to give in to the demands because if they refused, the regyabas would make a big scene. They would continue to praise the family and proclaim the household's good fortune, not leaving until their needs were satisfied.

There was another group, a second class of beggars, called the *pendongas*, who were responsible for keeping the streets clean and for disposing of the carcasses of dead animals. They helped other beggars in times of sickness and would also dispose of corpses, but only the corpses of beggars.

This hierarchy could be observed within the beggar community on many occasions. For instance, every morning we would leave a huge container of tsampa outside our house on the front doorstep, for the beggars to come and help themselves. It was the pendongas who oversaw the distribution of this tsampa. On those same special occasions when we received a visit from the regyabas, the pendongas would never be far behind. They would file into the courtyard and demand exactly half of what the regyabas had just received, and they would not leave unless we met their request. In their persistence they were certainly equal to the regyabas, but they would only ever ask for half as much.

A LIFE

KUNGA PELJOR

In our region of western Tibet there lived a district official from Lhasa. One day I was playing with some other children near this official's house while his wife was outside washing some clothes. She saw me in the large group of children and called me over. She gave me a sweet, asked my name, and said I was a good-looking boy. Soon afterwards, my father was invited to their house for the first of many meals. It turned out that the official's wife was unable to have children and, after a few meetings, this couple persuaded my parents, through some means, to give me up to them.

I wasn't told that I was being given to the official and his wife; my parents just said that I was to go and live with them as a servant. After a few days in their house, I developed a pain in my stomach and told the couple that I wanted to leave and be with my parents. "Don't worry, there is no need to go home," they said, and they gave me some Tibetan medicine and a massage to ease my pain. It really wasn't so bad being separated from my family, although when I went to bed at night I'd think of my mother and of everyone I knew, far away. Actually, I was treated with great kindness by this couple. My new mother would bathe me and give me massages with special creams that only the nobility could afford, warming her hands with her breath as she did this. It was very strange being bathed so many times. I thought maybe I smelt awful because my real family were nomads and we were always burning yak dung in our tent. I never cleaned myself like this when I was in our nomad camp, and now I was being bathed once a week! Another strange thing was that the official's wife used to come into my bed and sleep with me as if I were her baby.

In the beginning I had no idea I was to be their new child, but after a while I figured it out since servants were never treated like this. Being from a nomad family, I didn't know how to speak in proper Tibetan and they started to teach me the correct forms spoken by the nobility. I also began to learn many things about manners, such as how to serve and eat. As poor nomads, my family drank tea with only salt added to it, but now I was shown how to shake the teapot filled with butter tea—if we didn't shake it, all the butter would float to the top. I was also taught how to perform prayers, how to clean plates and cups, how to sweep, and how to serve the guests and high officials who came to our house. I remember how frightened I was when washing plates. I used to do it very slowly so they wouldn't slip out of my hands and break.

Although my real parents' camp was only a two-day journey from the official's house, I never saw my parents again. After two years, the official was transferred back to Lhasa, as his stay in our district had ended. Our journey to Lhasa took many days. The caravan had a great many horses and yaks, and there were eleven people, six of them servants. We carried large amounts of butter, which was being sent as a tax from our region to the government, and I rode on one of the yaks carrying this butter. Each day as we rode in the heat of the sun, the butter would melt and seep out of the stitches of the bags. I remember sticking my fingers into the butter and licking them as we went along.

Because my new parents held an important position in society, they wanted me to become a high official or serve under a prominent monk official, so when I was eleven years old they sent me to Sera Monastery to prepare for my future occupation. As a common monk, I spent most of my time studying the scriptures, with few other responsibilities. I was never very interested in book learning, and when I finally tired of it I

BEGGAR SEEKING ALMS, LHASA, TIBET

became a dob-dob to free myself from study. I worked as a tea server and, like other members of this community, became responsible for enforcing discipline. Then, at the age of nineteen, I visited my stepparents' house for a New Year's party and picnic. Many relatives and neighbors had been invited, and among the crowd I noticed a very pretty girl. Her cheeks were red and her hair was beautiful. At that time I was young and quite handsome. She was a little older than I was, and she was staring at me quite a lot; I could not take my eyes off her, either. We talked for a bit and then, while all the guests were sitting in the main room, we slipped out and went into the storage room and made love.

I had broken my vows and in my heart and mind I knew I could no longer remain a monk. Shortly afterwards my stepparents talked with the girl's family and learned what had happened. I immediately ran away from both the monastery and my family, leaving without any food, not even tsampa or cheese. All I had were the lay clothes I was wearing and a little money in my pocket. I started to wander from monastery to monastery, visiting many holy places along the way. The money, however, didn't last long, and my poverty forced me to continue my journey as a beggar.

In the beginning I was very shy and had no experience in asking for alms. When I was courageous enough to ask for something, most people gave me tsampa, tea, or a little chang. Over time I became more bold and would call out, "Please mother, give me tsampa," and things like that. The very first time I was given anything was when I was sitting in front of a house owned by a wealthy family. After I had sat there for about three hours not saying a word, an old man came out and asked me what I was doing sitting there for so long. I told him that I had run away from my monastery in Lhasa and that I didn't have any food. He gave me tsampa and other things to eat. He also gave me a bowl to eat from, a blanket, and a pair of shoes, because the soles of my own shoes had worn through. After hearing my story he advised, "Don't roam around like this. You seem to be from a good family." But I was determined to continue my wanderings and so I traveled on.

Although I met many beggars, I didn't want to be with them. Many simply had no desire to work, which is why they took to begging. Because I was very young at the time, some of the beggars advised me not to live like this, and said I was giving my family a bad name. Other beggars pointed out which households were most generous, the places where there was an angry dog, and the families that were known for being very stingy. They also taught me that when I called out, "Mother, please!" I should make the words sound long, like "pleeeease. . . ."

At night I often slept in piles of straw stored in separate buildings near a farmer's house. If I arrived early, I would ask permission and might be given a bowl of soup, but if I arrived late, then I'd just go to sleep there without asking. Most people were very kind and didn't scold me for living like this; I don't recall anyone being cruel. In the wintertime I'd usually go to a big family and work for them, taking care of the animals in return for food and a place to stay. Many of them asked me to stay on and work for them permanently, but I thought that if I did I would probably never see my stepparents again. Always in the back of my mind there was the thought that my mother and father were very angry with me and that it would take time for them to cool down.

When I reached Sakya Monastery a number of monks tried to convince me to return to the monastic life. They were very forceful in their arguments, so I told them about having had sex and that this was why I couldn't return. If I hadn't told them, I'm sure that to this day they would still be trying to get me back in monk's robes.

On my pilgrimage I went to Tashilhunpo Monastery to receive a blessing from the Panchen Lama. He was not there at the time; instead I received blessings from other high lamas and from a famous relic. I sought these blessings because I knew I had done wrong and had broken my monk's vows. My constant prayer was for forgiveness as I traveled on my way, reciting "Om Mani Padme Hum."

Sakya was a very good area and in all I spent two years there. For a small amount of tsampa you could get a quarter of a dried goat or sheep—a very good deal! During that time, I worked for farmers and sometimes as a cook's helper in the monasteries, cleaning the kitchen utensils and so forth. I served the monks and lamas their food and tea, which was work I enjoyed.

On my travels I met many women; quite a few asked me to stay but I always said I couldn't. After wandering for four years, I finally returned to Lhasa to see my stepparents. They scolded me, saying, "You have done bad things. We worried about whether you were alive or not," but then they calmed down and were happy to see me. The young woman had waited for me, all those years. She came to live in our house and became my wife. We had children—a boy and a girl—but we only had five years together. When the Chinese invaded I joined the "Four Rivers and Six Mountains" guerrilla force, and from then on I was fighting and fleeing from the Chinese army until I escaped to India. I never saw my wife or our children again.

After experiencing many different levels of Tibetan society and leaving behind so much, I feel the happiest time in my life was when I traveled and lived as a beggar. I was not dependent upon others, and I never had any worries.

[MUSLIM NEIGHBORS]

TSERING DOLKAR YUTHOK

I knew quite a number of Muslim families in Lhasa. When I was twelve, I had two Muslim girlfriends who sometimes took me to the mosque. They would sneak me in so I could watch them doing their prostrations and praying. Inside the mosque were two slabs of stone set in the ground at an angle; I didn't know what they were for, but they had something to do with praying. However, as any child might do, I just climbed on one of them and used it as a slide.

The Muslims in Lhasa were gentle people who knew how to live well, taking many breaks during the summertime and leaving Lhasa for their favorite picnic regions outside the city. They were very friendly and related well to people outside their own community. Different nationalities made up the Muslim community—there were Chinese, Nepalis, Kashmiris, and Ladakhis. Some of the Kashmiris, descendants of traders who had settled in Tibet, had Tibetan wives. A Tibetan woman who married a Muslim would convert to Islam, and the children would be considered Muslim. She would wear a scarf on her head, but apart from that she dressed exactly the same as other Tibetan women. The Chinese Muslims were considered to be a separate group within the community because of their race, and they usually married among themselves. But this was the only difference, and there were strong friendships among us all.

The area where I grew up had Muslim families who had lived there for many generations, and there were friendships between our families that had been passed on from one generation to the next. My friends and I were very close, and the fact that I was Buddhist and my friends were Muslim was of no consequence to us. We grew up together like brothers and sisters, having the same experiences. We often visited each other's

RECITING PRAYERS IN A MONASTERY COURTYARD, MANALI, INDIA

YOUNG NOMAD WOMAN, N.E. AMDO PROVINCE, TIBET

76

homes, and the only difference I can remember was that when Muslim friends came to visit they could not eat certain foods. For example, as a guest at a meal they would eat butter, tsampa, and cheese, but not meat. Even though the meat had been butchered by a Muslim, it would not have been done according to their religious code, so they could not eat it. However, when I went to a Muslim friend's house I would eat everything. On the day of the Muslim New Year, our friends would bring us a huge plate of their special celebration meal—a type of pulao rice with a lot of meat, raisins, and yogurt.

The Muslim community was very strict about their religious duties. They prayed five times a day, and the men were always checking the time to make sure they did not miss one of their prayer times. When I visited my friends' homes, I would see the women drop whatever they were doing and leave to do their prayers and prostrations. On Fridays the whole community went to the big mosque just outside the area where the Chinese and Kashmiris lived. They did not mix religions and would never go to the Jokhang Temple—that's why it was such an adventure for my childhood friends when I sneaked them in.

The families we knew were mostly business people, traders who traveled to India and China and brought back goods to sell in Tibet. Muslims were known to have good business sense and were admired for their ability to organize themselves. The wealthier Muslims would do the traveling, buying all sorts of items—makeup, beads, needles, fabric, even material from Italy that they found in India. On their return they would sell the goods wholesale to other Muslims, the shopkeepers and street sellers, who sold them on the market. The shopkeepers of the Barkhor market district were famous for their eloquent speech. Of the many regional dialects in Tibet, the purest spoken form of the language is the Lhasa dialect, of which the most beautiful form is the Barkhor dialect spoken in the market. The shopkeepers, most of them Muslim, were greatly admired for being able to speak so well.

Most Muslims were involved in business. Many of them were butchers and they supplied meat to all of Lhasa. One of the families I knew was responsible for supplying meat to the Potala kitchens. The animals were butchered in one area and then the meat was taken to an open market to be sold. Once in a while I went to this meat market, which was always very crowded, and to the flea market next to it, where you could find all sorts of things, from trinkets to expensive jewelry. Some of the butchers' families had walls around their houses made of yak bones and horns, mixed with mud. As a child, I found it quite frightening to walk past these walls.

When I visited Lhasa with one of my daughters in 1986, I looked around and found many changes. As I passed in front of the mosque where I had played as a child, I saw an old woman sitting on the ground selling cigarettes. Somehow I recognized her as one of my Muslim girlfriends who had taken me into the mosque to play, so long ago. She then realized who I was, too, and we both cried. Some things survive despite the changes.

MUSLIM NEIGHBOR, AMDO PROVINCE, TIBET

Nomad Reading Buddhist Texts, Kalachakra Initiation, Jispa, Lahaul, India

ARCHERY CONTEST, STOK MONASTERY, LADAKH, INDIA

TORMA MAKER, MERU NYINGBA MONASTERY, LHASA, TIBET

PERPETUAL TURNING OF A PRAYER WHEEL, POTALA PALACE, LHASA, TIBET

PLAYING LONG HORNS AS PILGRIMS PASS BELOW, TASHILHUNPO MONASTERY, TIBET

MAKING LONG HORNS

JAMYANG SAKYA

Tibetan long horns are called *thongchen* or *radong*. They are always played in pairs by two monks. Until meeting my husband, Sakya Rinpoche, I had only seen long horns in use at the monastery, but Rinpoche loved them and wanted to learn the proper way to play. Also, since he was to be a teacher of monks, he needed to learn about the horns and every other aspect of Buddhist rituals. So I learned firsthand just how large and heavy long horns are and how hard they are to play. Blowing the horns is so difficult that it stretches the inside of your mouth. Also, you can't play them in a house because of the volume of sound, though sometimes Rinpoche practiced upstairs in the summer palace. Other times, he practiced outside for hours, sometimes in the cold winter; even when his mouth was bleeding, he would continue to play.

When we went to eastern Tibet, my husband made arrangements for eight of these long horns to be made—four pairs. The metals came from many sources. I had been collecting used gold, silver, and jewelry since we arrived in Kham. Some patrons and monks had also contributed. The nomad people and the people of Menyag offered Rinpoche gifts of their own silver and gold jewelry. When they saw him, they would take their jewelry off there and then and offer it to him. By so doing, the giver would accumulate merit. We also melted down old Chinese coins and silver money. Eventually we had boxes and boxes of precious metals; with these Rinpoche was able to provide for the making of the eight long horns.

It took about eight or ten months for eighteen blacksmiths in a monastery in eastern Tibet to make the long horns. The craftsmen were the famous smiths of the Derge area of Kham. We also arranged with these experts to make dozens of other musical and religious instruments including both long and short trumpets, about a thousand butter lamp containers made of molded silver, and other religious things such as charm boxes and offering cups. All these objects, except the lamp containers, were made from a base of silver or copper and had gold-plated designs over quicksilver.

The head of the smiths was an older and highly experienced man. He was very religious and would rise early to pray. While working he often mumbled mantras. The other smiths were all young, under thirty. Many were descended from generations of artisans and, as craftsmen, they all commanded respect. The Lhagyal monks helped them, working nine to ten hours a day around three charcoal-fueled stoves in the courtyard. It was summertime, and the courtyard was noisy with the pounding of metal. When it was too hot, tents were erected to shade the smiths. Buttermilk was served to cool them, and they ate four meals a day. I went to the courtyard frequently to survey their progress. It was fun to observe the construction, and I learned much about this ancient craft.

The smiths first would make a design and then show it to my husband for final approval. Then the metals would be melted down in small clay pots. The completed objects were kept in a large room on the second floor of the palace. This storage room was also used to complete the drying of the pieces. To ensure that the handicraft was not damaged, raw wool was placed on the floor, then blankets, and finally cotton flannel.

When each major set of pieces was completed, we held a large meal for the whole group, and each smith received a gift of extra food—a dried leg of lamb, big pastries, or dried fruits—that he saved to take home later. Sometimes there were also gifts of clothing. I sent to Lharigar for Chinese-made vodka, which came in barrels, for their parties, as

One time during Monlam, the Great Prayer Festival that took place right after Tibetan New Year, I was with a group of fourteen dob-dobs roaming around Lhasa. On this occasion, we were having a picnic near a military camp and I was still a junior member of the community. Two sentries were not happy to see us passing so near them and going up and down the same road as the camp. Perhaps we looked arrogant, as dob-dobs often do. The sentries began calling us *barkors*—meaning monks without vows. This was a real insult. I grabbed one of the soldiers' guns and hit him on the shoulder with the rifle butt. He stumbled, but then picked up his gun and ran away with the other soldiers. That evening we returned to our monastery, happy that there were no signs of any consequences from this encounter.

Three days later, we returned to the same spot to continue our picnic. Now, you have to understand that during the Monlam festival the army had no power or authority over monks—the only authority was the discipline committee of Drepung Monastery. The commander of the army wrote to this committee and asked it to exert some control over us, telling the committee that we had beaten some soldiers and that there would be clashes if nothing were done about our fight. When the authorities at the monastery learned of our actions, it became a very big issue and they sent about sixty people to search for us. We were in a house at the picnic grounds when I noticed a group of monks with many high officials coming toward us. We jumped up from our beds and blocked the door. While five of us held the door, the other nine hid wherever they could, some in the storage area where dung cakes were kept, and others jumped into large leather bags. Once they were hidden we opened the door and said that we had not done anything unlawful. The five of us were immediately arrested and taken to a prison, where we were kept two to a cell. It was very dark in the cells, but because we were young we had no fear at all. That night we were taken out of our cells and lined up before a powerful group of our teachers, house masters, discipline committee members, and the head of all the dob-dobs.

We soon became quite frightened when they placed before us a huge pan containing a blazing fire. Into this fire they put blessed grains called *chanay*. The purpose of this ceremony was to bring out our moral conscience—to put the fear of God into us, you might say. Even with this we did not reveal the names of the others. Then they began to beat us with a thick stick. The head of the dob-dobs gave each of us three hundred lashes on the buttocks. No one uttered a word, but then my turn came. I was a little younger than the rest and I heard the command that I should be beaten with great force and with a stick that was a little thinner than the one used to beat the others. You see, a thinner stick would produce greater pain. "He will come out with the names," they said. "He will surely break down." When I heard this, I put my robe in my mouth and took all three hundred lashes without saying a word. The assembly was very surprised, but they still wanted to know the names, so they ordered that I be given fifty more lashes. Although my flesh was badly cut and bleeding, I still said nothing—none of us spoke a word. We did not even cry out since that would have been a disgrace.

After this we had a good reputation for not revealing the names of the others. It was natural for the monks in our monastery to be impressed and pleased with our loyalty to each other. When I was a young dob-dob I was involved in many minor fights and petty misbehaviors, but this fight during Monlam was the most memorable. When I turned twenty-five—a year in one's life when it is believed that one encounters obstacles and accidents—I was very careful for the whole year and, after that, I stopped being a problem to others. Some years after our encounter with the army, I became the head of the dob-dob community. The position was granted based on the respect I had gained from this fight and because I was now a senior member of our community. I held this position for seven years, during which time I was quite successful with discipline and in looking after the welfare of the community. Before this, the community was quite poor, so I thought I should improve their condition. Because we needed lots of money, it was my idea to go out into the villages to the wealthy families and build houses for them. This worked well, and in return we were given land, fields to cultivate, and, from the sale of the crops, we earned money. We also organized picnics outside the monastery area, where our sponsors and wealthy families could come to gamble, from which we also earned money. Over time the fearsome reputation of the dob-dobs turned to respect.

PAYBACK

LOBSANG GYALTSO

When I was twenty-one years old, three years after I entered the monastery in Lhasa, I had a friend who was a senior monk. One day a medium-sized bag of tsampa disappeared from my room, which at that time I never locked. So, for a few days I had no tsampa to eat and I went around trying to find out who had taken it. After a while the bag of tsampa reappeared, back in its proper place. I suspected this senior monk of the prank. Hiding a monk's property was a common prank we played among ourselves. Another was to go into a friend's room when he was preparing some food for himself and, when he went out of the room, eat everything in the pot, even while it was still cooking. We did a lot of things like this. For example, there was a trick we played with sticks from salt bags. In Tibet salt comes in large cloth sacks that are closed by gathering the top of the bag and piercing it with a small wooden stick that is pointed at both ends and smooth all around, like a pencil. We would sometimes place these little sticks on a staircase, and then whoever stepped on them would fall down some stairs and get a few bruises. I played this trick on several older monks because I had a grudge against them.

One day, a few months after my tsampa disappeared, I went to visit my older friend in his room. It was unlocked and he was nowhere to be seen, so I thought I'd pay him back for his trick on me. I collected some of his valuable things and hid them in another monk's room. Much later I learned that this senior monk soon guessed that I was to blame, and together with some other monks he thought of a way of teaching me a lesson. A few days after hiding these things I went to his room to check on how the trick was working. When I arrived, there were some friends of his there. He was rolling up a *khata* (an offering scarf) in a sheet of paper and, as he did this, he told me that a terrible thing had happened—a large amount of money had been taken from his shrine box. "There must have been a thief in my room," he said. "I will have to report it to the officials in the great prayer hall and they'll announce it to the main gathering of monks." He went on to say that he'd give the thief three days to replace the money in the box, exactly as it was before, and that if this were done he wouldn't inform the authorities.

Of course, there had been no large amount of money in the box—in fact there had probably been no money at all—but all I knew at the time was that I was implicated in the affair and I had no way of putting back this large sum of money. He insisted several times that he didn't care about the property or any of the items, but he had to have the money back. Now I knew that if the authorities in the main temple were informed of the incident it would be extremely serious because of the huge sum he had mentioned. It would mean jail or, at the very least, a severe beating with sticks. This senior monk and his friends were all looking at me as if to say, "Oh, this is a very bad situation; this is not a normal incident at all." I could see that they suspected me.

Over the next few days I was so upset I couldn't sleep. Finally I decided it would be best if I confessed. So I went and told the senior monk that I had taken his things and hidden them, but that I hadn't taken any money. He said, "Well, that's one thing, but why didn't you lock the box after you took things? Later on, someone must have come along and stolen all the money. You're really going to be in trouble for what you did." There was another senior monk there and he agreed, adding that if only I could catch the thief and recover the money then everything would be OK, but if I couldn't then I'd be in a very serious position.

For the next five or six days they kept demanding that I find the thief. Every night I was sleepless and filled with worry. I became more and more sick at heart. Then this group of monks got together again and called me to my friend's room. They said that now there was no option but to give my name to the authorities. They asked if I had any other ideas. In deep depression I replied that since I had not been able to catch the thief, I'd try to replace all of the money slowly, bit by bit. They were very surprised by this and immediately burst out laughing. "You have a small mind," they said. "If you couldn't go through with it, then you shouldn't have started to play with us." It all suddenly became very clear.

This was one occasion—perhaps the only one—when I was the loser from a practical joke. The senior monk was nomad Pema Chonze; after this incident, whenever I used to scold other monks they'd say I needed another lesson from Pema Chonze and that he was the only one who could outsmart me. After this I never hid another monk's property. In fact, I think it was the last big trick I ever played.

MONK STUDYING AT SHRINE ROOM DOOR, LOCATION UNKNOWN, TIBET

Monks Enjoying Losar Celebrations, Sera Monastery, Bylakuppe, India

MONKS RUNNING THROUGH STUPAS, TASHIDING MONASTERY, SIKKIM, INDIA

NUNS AT MONASTERY KITCHEN DOOR, DOLMA LING NUNNERY, DHARAMSALA AREA, INDIA

A GOOD PLACE TO MEET

NGAWANGTHONGDUP NARKYID

In Lhasa, a good place for a girl and a boy to meet and make their arrangements was the central market area called the Barkhor. It was here, every evening just before sunset, that people gathered to circumambulate the Jokhang Temple and pass by the many shops that lined the route. People would walk around, then maybe sit and watch the passersby or go into the Jokhang to make offerings and look at the holy statues.

Young people also met each other at the many yearly festivals, especially at the summer picnic that took place on the fifteenth day of the fifth month of the Tibetan year. During the day of the full moon there would be a fire *puja* to clean and purify the whole world. This picnic was a very good time for meeting, playing together, and getting to know each other because for two weeks thousands of people lived all along the river in tents. Parents would tell their sons and daughters, "Watch. This is your chance to look around and see who you like."

One of the best times in the year to meet and be together was during the harvest. People said that the evening sky during harvest was so bright that you could almost see well enough to write. The autumn moon is huge and low in the sky, and we would say that the Goddess of the Moon had come down to provide light to help the farmers and nomads so that they could work late into the night. At harvest time there are large piles of straw in the fields, and between these piles there are many private places where young girls and boys can go to meet while everyone else is working and singing. The harvest songs are often about love. By listening to these songs, working, and eating together, young farmers and nomads meet and become attracted to each other.

For Tibetans there is little tension around sexuality. Everything is quite relaxed, although we don't talk openly about sex in public and, even if men and women have very strong desires for each other, they never touch in public. Normally girls are a bit shy. Even if a girl loves a man, she tends to express this through shyness. In preparing for lovemaking, for instance, she wouldn't remove her own clothes; the boy must do this. Nomads and farmers, in particular, are very shy; the girls among the town aristocracy are more open and frank. Sometimes, though, the boy forces the girl; this was known to happen.

There were "free" marriages based on love and there were many songs written about this. Other marriages were brought about by "accidents," which could occur quite easily. For instance, down by the river where everyone went to do the washing, there were always a lot of people milling around and, amid the joking and playing, two young people might disappear into the nearby trees and there would be an "accident."

Although free marriage was practiced in many different sectors of Tibetan society—in Lhasa, in the villages, and even among the nomads—under some circumstances such marriages were less acceptable. For example, when a lama wanted to marry a woman from a lower class, people tended to disapprove, so the lama would say that the woman was in fact a *dakini*, a female celestial being. Now, I'm not a very good Tibetan, and unlike most Tibetans I'm rather critical—but in my opinion, the real reason why many lamas say they have met a dakini is that it's an excuse and actually they've fallen in love! A family might invite a lama to their house to officiate at all their family rituals. He may see the daughter often; she's beautiful, he falls in love, and then he uses religion to explain his desire! There might be a big age gap between the lama and the young girl, but he'll just say, "Ah, but she is a dakini and very pure."

During our time as students at the Potala there were two young women, whom one could meet outside the walls of Shol village, who would sleep with men. Everybody knew this. This wasn't a case of paying money for sex. It wasn't like that; we didn't have prostitution like in the West. It was just that if these women wanted to, they would sleep with the man. Similarly, in the center of Lhasa, there were places where men and women could get together, like chang halls, where they'd decide on where to go to make love. The man might give a gift of cloth or ornaments to the woman, and sometimes she would even give him a gift.

In Tibet two men who were brothers, relatives, or close friends would often hold hands or walk along holding each other, but this had nothing to do with sexuality. The same was true for women and girls. I did, however, hear of the existence of homosexual practices both in the military and in the monasteries. In Tibet these relations were not between grown men; usually there was a big difference in age. In terms of sexual enjoyment, the usual practice was for the younger male, being still smooth-skinned, to cross his legs and keep his thighs tightly pressed together. The older man could then make use of this smooth place. You see, all monks make a vow not to engage in sex that involves any part of the body that is a "hole"—a mouth, anus, or vagina—so this was a way around that vow.

There was a game that some young monks, boys, used to play together, usually while bathing in the river. It involved masturbating into each other's arm pits, competing to see who could retain their sperm the longest. Some had total control, keeping the sperm inside and not eject-ing it at all. This was all said to be good preparation for tantric practice! There would be bets, as well; for instance, the first boy to lose control would have to offer tea and food to everybody. None of this was hidden. Everybody was there, bathing together, and they would agree, "Okay, let's have a competition." Afterwards the bets were settled: "He lost, I won. He has to serve everyone."

Monks were well known for always talking about sex, telling dirty stories, and teasing nuns as well as each other. We used to say that the monk's mouth was the most foul thing about him, and we'd tease the nuns by saying that, because the nun must use her finger a lot, the dirtiest thing about a nun was her finger. There was also a certain joke about nuns, although it can't be true because it's certainly impossible! We used to say that two nuns would get a boiled egg that was "as long as possible" and put it between their private parts, and then both would rub this way and that, moving together. This was a well-known joke, so we'd buy raw eggs in the market and wait for a nun to come through the crowd. We'd greet her respectfully, bowing with our hands pressed together. The egg would be hidden between our hands and then we'd say, "I have something to give you," and put the egg in her hand. The nun would usually let out a surprised "EEEE!" and show some anger, saying "Bad boys!" or something. Then we'd run—otherwise the nun would throw the egg at us, if she, in a state of shock, hadn't already dropped it on the ground. Everybody in the market would laugh since they all knew the meaning of the joke.

TIBETAN COUPLE, DARJEELING, INDIA

MONKEY RIDING A FOX

RINZIN WANGYAL

I have been trained as a *nyawo*. This is the person who, on behalf of the boy's family, goes from the boy's house to the girl's house to ask for her hand in marriage. The girl's household also has a representative called a *dhokla gompo*, and each marriage ceremony involves many songs and formal debates between these two. My grandfather and my uncle were nyawos and I learned the nyawo's duties from them. I, in turn, have taught this ceremony to two or three other men. All the songs and questions and answers used in this tradition can be found in one text; over time this book has been reduced from eighteen chapters to nine, and then from nine to three.

One of my first duties as a nyawo begins after a father has chosen a girl who he thinks will make a good wife for his son. The father and I will approach the girl's family at most three times. If they haven't accepted our proposal by the third visit, there won't be a marriage. The days on which we make our offer will be decided by an astrologer. On our first visit we bring some chang and a sum of money wrapped in a clean white scarf. The girl's family doesn't usually accept in the beginning, and they put us off with various excuses: that they must ask the girl or they must call their relatives to the tent and discuss whether this is a good match. If the family really does not want to accept then they return the chang and scarf; but if they want to think about it they will often say, "Just leave them here between us and we will discuss matters." If either parent accepts and the other refuses, I go to the parent who has refused and offer a scarf and try to convince him or her that this is a good proposal.

If the girl's family accepts, then the day of marriage is chosen by the nyawo, based on the ages of the boy and girl. Once this date is fixed, the girl's house requests that the boy's family offer them and all their relatives

a ceremony of tea and chang. As I serve these drinks and sing special songs, I also offer a white scarf to each family member. On the first day there are also many other songs—for example, those sung while prayer flags are put on the doors and the pillars of the boy's house in preparation for the visit by the girl's family. During a chang offering—called "Discussion Chang"—the dhokla and I discuss who, and how many, will come to the marriage. To each of those invited, a prayer flag is sent, wrapped around a small piece of tea cut from a tea brick.

This visit, and the ones that follow, involve so many songs that if I told you them all, this would never end. So I will mention only one or two from the second and third days' ceremonies—even though, when this three-day ceremony is performed, no part is ever left out.

On the second day, as we go to the girl's house, I sing a song of how there are five horsemen—the nyawo, the nyawo's helper, and so on. In the song, each of us rides in a particular way, reflecting the spirit whence we come—the water spirit, the earth spirit, and so on—but the sixth horse, which we bring for the girl to ride, comes from our human realm.

On arriving, I sing a song to the lama who is there saying prayers for the girl's family and then a song to the mandala he has before him. After these I explain, in song, the meaning of the things that I am carrying: an arrow, a wool spindle, a type of prayer wheel with the pictures of twelve animals inside, and finally a butter lamp. For example, the song about the prayer wheel and animals has to do with averting obstacles and problems. After singing about each object, I give it to the lama, but if I get one of these songs wrong, then the lama doesn't accept the object.

After addressing the lama, I turn to the dhokla, who is also waiting for me outside the girl's house with his own songs and questions. First we sing about meeting each other. In my song I say that I have come from far away and have crossed many passes, putting prayer flags on these passes; that we have crossed valleys where there are many bandits, traveling through dry deserts, "to meet you, dhokla"; and I give him a scarf. Then the dhokla replies, singing that yesterday he dimly saw some horsemen, "but this evening I see that the horsemen are like monkeys, the horses like foxes, bringing for the girl a horse that looks like a sheep. The arrow you carry, nyawo, is like a broom, and the bow is like the stick we use to push cow dung into the cooking fire. Monkey who rides a fox, where are you going?" I sing in reply that it is not possible for a monkey to ride a fox. "You should not say such things. You should respect us as humans. The horses come from the deity and from the spirit of the earth, of the water. . . . We have come from a long distance to take the girl back."

After this debating, which can go on sometimes for a whole day, I must sing a song for each of the eighty stones that the dhokla has set up near the gate of the girl's house. These songs are explanations for each stone; once each song is sung I kick the stone over with my foot. If I do not know, or forget, a particular song, then I must give a scarf to the dhokla. At the first white stone the dhokla says that it is a dog, asking, "Why is there smoke coming from its nose and fire from its mouth? Why is he standing on four legs, and why is his tail like wool?" I sing in response that the smoke is like a misty steam as from one's breath on a cold day, the fire is like lightning, and the white tail is an omen of the snow.

Passing now to the third day, when the girl departs from her family, it is the duty of the nyawo to sing a song as the girl leaves—"This is your birthplace, but you don't have a right to stay. You must now go to another place to spend your life." After a very short distance I sing another song, this time to the girl's family, saying, "No matter what you did, I've been successful in getting your daughter from you." After this, the lama prays that the family's wealth not be lost with the going of the girl. There is also a lama waiting outside of the boy's house when we finally arrive. He then chants prayers in front of the girl to dispel the bad omens or influences that some Tibetans believe arrive with a new wife.

Inside the house, the ceremony of the arrow and spindle begins again, this time addressed to the boy's family by the dhokla from the girl's family. The same sitting songs and rice and chang songs follow, of which there are forty-eight; seven different utensils are used in this ceremony, and, as before, the songs explain the meaning of each item. Then I give one cup of chang and one plate of tsampa to the couple and sing that this food comes from the deity and that we pray that they will have a long and good life. The couple then eat together. Thirteen different songs end the third day of the marriage ceremony. During all these ceremonies and songs the marriage bed is being prepared, often in a special and separate tent.

On the fourth day the family members and guests all gather for feasting and celebrations. Relatives and friends bring offerings of food to the home of the family that invited them. The meat, butter, chang, and other foods are now prepared, and the feast goes on until all has been eaten—often taking two or three days—during which time the two families dance, talk, and sing, united through the newly married couple.

ASTROLOGY

DAKTHDUN JAMPA GYELTSEN

Oddly enough, I began to study astrology purely out of curiosity, since it had no relation to what my inherited position as a government official would require of me. After completing my early education in Lhasa, I returned to my stately home and continued studies in Tibetan grammar, poetry, and literature with tutors selected by my family. One of these instructors was asked by many of his students to teach the subject of astrology, and he asked me if I also wanted to learn this complex science. So it was under these circumstances that I was introduced to astrology at about the age of seventeen. Not unlike a man being thrust into a new and unknown country, I felt both confused and curious about the significance of the movement of the planets and stars. Nevertheless, as I was constantly reminded, my major studies were preparing me for the civil service.

When I turned twenty-one, my life changed completely. It was 1959, and the Chinese army had invaded Tibet. My duty was to fight the Chinese, since our government and entire way of life were in crisis. The Tibetan resistance movement was unsuccessful in defeating the invading forces, and I became a hunted man. In order to save my life I escaped into exile through Bhutan. My father remained behind in Tibet. Because he was a government official, he was thrown in prison, where he eventually died. I arrived in Bhutan empty-handed, yet I had to make a living. Since the Bhutanese had a great interest in astrology, I started preparing horoscopes to earn some money.

Tibetan people were very dependent on astrology, as many are today, and they believed that everything was guided by it. The head of a household would consult astrological signs for even the smallest aspects of his or her life. For instance, if a person wanted to go to the top of a local hill to perform an incense-burning ceremony, he would consult an astrologer to see if a particular day was auspicious or not. Even in the villages, if the head of the family could read a little bit, he would know something about astrology.

As soon as a Tibetan was born, a horoscope was made. Since the birth was usually at home, astrology was used to determine on which day the child could first be taken outside of the house. Every aspect of life was determined and governed by the stars. Tibet has a very harsh climate and washing one's hair is considered a very important task, so astrology was used to determine when this should be done.

When it came to marriage, both the boy's and the girl's charts were brought to the astrologer to be compared and studied. Making a marriage horoscope was determined by the Tibetan way of life. A man's responsibility involved the outside world, making a living, facing an enemy, and protecting the household. When calculating a man's chart, the astrologer would place a greater emphasis on those aspects relating to life force and success. Since a woman was mostly concerned with the home, family, and domestic affairs, it was most important to determine what the horoscope indicated about her health and wealth.

Now, if a family decided that they wanted their daughter's husband to become a member of their own household, then the bride's chart became very important. The girl's family would collect the horoscopes of all the boys who were being considered as possible husbands, and compare them to their daughter's to see which would make the best match. Greater importance was always placed on the horoscope of the young person whose family received the partner into their household.

When there are astrological differences in the portion of a chart

ASLEEP IN A NOMAD'S TENT, SUMED TIBETAN NOMAD CAMP, LADAKH, INDIA

relating to health, illness can arise. If there is a clash in fortunes, financial misfortunes may occur. An astrologer may recommend the saying of certain prayers, or the wearing of special talismans or amulets. Often the astrologer is consulted in times of sickness. By studying the patient's horoscope, the astrologer can determine the correct prayers and religious practices needed to treat the sick person.

Death is the final journey that a person takes in this life; when an individual dies, his body is not touched until the astrologer is consulted. This was sometimes a problem because there might not be an astrologer living nearby, and it could be days before one was found and brought to the site of the corpse. The astrologer was asked to make calculations, based on when the death occurred, to determine in which direction the body should be moved and when the cremation or burial should take place.

An astrologer will study a person's chart in order to prescribe certain antidotes or solutions to the difficulties that arise in that person's life. In Tibet, people often had to make long journeys through barren and unpopulated lands. They usually carried a religious text that told them which day was dedicated to which deity. When, for example, they had stomach pains or some other affliction, they would consult this sacred text. For that particular day, the text might advise them that, to solve their problem, they should sit and take their tsampa, add some salt, and make an offering toward the east.

According to many old stories, after a crime was committed, an astrologer who was very skilled and did his calculations with great accuracy could pinpoint the dishonest person. But according to Tibetan law, if the accused denied the crime, then both had to be beaten if the astrologer could provide no other proof. Because of this risk, astrologers purposely avoided these kinds of calculations.

Once after the government had printed a new banknote, the printers, in their excitement, quickly took these new bills to the bank for distribution without first consulting an astrological chart. They learned later that they had made their delivery of the money on a very inauspicious day. After that, Tibetan people treated this valuable note as unlucky: they thought it was too easy to spend, and believed that it would be used to buy things one didn't want.

I am not very familiar with Western astrology, but there is a belief in some schools that the stars and planets have a direct, causal effect on our lives and that there is no way to escape it. Our Tibetan approach to astrology has been totally influenced by the teachings of the Buddha. There is always cause and effect. We are responsible for whatever actions we perform, and things can be changed. It is like sowing a seed: if nothing is done to change the development of the seed, then the seed may or may not grow. But we believe that there are things or actions that can be done to help the seed break through. There are remedies that can be used to change the course of events. One of the basic tenets of Buddhist teaching is that if a wrong is done, then it is possible to correct it through sincere acts of atonement, but wrong attitudes such as arrogance could reverse the process. It is not the stars and planets that ultimately determine our destiny.

PILGRIM ARRIVING AT A HOT SPRING AND NUNNERY, TERDROM NUNNERY AND CHUTSEN CHUGANG HOT SPRINGS, TIBET

VISITING THE WATERS

TSERING DOLKAR YUTHOK

In southern Tibet at Pembo there is a hot spring where the water flows between two large rocks shaped like elephant heads that were said to have been miraculously self-created. It's up in the mountains, about three days on horseback from Lhasa and three hours from the nearest village. People say that the great religious teacher Tsong Khapa discovered this spring when he was a wandering hermit. While bathing, he leaned against the side of the spring to rest, and left an impression of the shape of his back and head in the rock. People believed in the healing power of this spot, and everyone tried to fit their backs into Tsong Khapa's sacred imprint when they went in to bathe.

There are two pools, one hot and one cold. The hot water comes from under the mountain and it's really hot at the source—you can burn yourself if you dip your hand in too near the opening. The water is considered to be very holy. Those who are sick will recover if they bathe in it, unless they are so seriously ill that their life force is too weak. It's not for all kinds of disease—usually people with pains in their legs and joints bathed there. Right above the source is a stone where the cold water comes out, just a few drops at a time. This water, which we called Tara's milk, is very cold and slightly white, and bathers used to drink it for its healing properties.

There was a caretaker in charge of the spring who would call people to bathe—once in the morning and once in the evening. No fee was charged for using the spring, though some people made offerings to the caretaker. Of course, since Tibetans are quite modest, the men, women, and monks all bathed at different times. The pool could hold about fifteen people, although it was said that any number could enter the water and there would be room for all. When I went there were four to ten women bathing at a time. People usually bathed for an hour, but some people couldn't stay long in the water as it made them feel weak and dizzy. It's important to eat and drink well to avoid such problems, so after the evening bath the adults would drink a cup of very good chang.

I visited the hot spring twice, the first time when I was eleven. My brother and I accompanied my father, who was having problems with his legs—they were swollen and covered with black patches. His doctor came to the spring with us and directed the treatment. If things were going well, my father bathed twice a day; otherwise he took breaks, depending on the doctor's instructions. After about a month there, his condition improved, and on our return to Lhasa he continued his medical treatment and soon recovered completely.

My second visit, when I was twenty-eight, was for relaxation, as my first husband, Wangdu Sonam Dhongonpa, had recently died. I was accompanied by relatives and servants, and since it was summertime we traveled slowly, visiting monasteries on the way. It's very beautiful when you reach the spring; you climb a small hill, which is flat on top, and there it is. Near the spring are many small animals, and yellow mushrooms grow all around. We used to collect the mushrooms, stuff them with tsampa and butter and roast them over a fire. This was considered a great delicacy. A lot of people, perhaps seventy or eighty from all levels of society, camped in tents around the spring. Their yaks and horses were kept at nearby villages and farms or sent up into the mountains with the nomads. Sometimes, to accumulate merit, a family would prepare a huge meal at the caretaker's house, then invite the entire assembly to join the feast.

This was such a beautiful mountain, all grass and fields. I remember when I was on my first visit there as a child, and my brother and I were playing above the spring. We were running around, chasing a small animal called an *abbra*. That night, when everyone was sleeping, a snow leopard came down into the camp. We could hear it walking around, circling the tents, and growling. I was really scared, but I was told to be quiet or else the leopard would come inside the tent. It went to our servants' tent, and I could hear it clawing at the yak-hair covering. These tents are very strong and thick, so fortunately it didn't get in.

The next morning the whole camp was talking about it. The leopard had made so much noise growling and clawing at the tents that it woke up just about everyone. My brother and I received a severe scolding. We were told not to chase animals because it was disturbing the guardian spirits of the mountain. The abbra in particular should not be molested, they told me, adding that if I did it again, the leopard would return and eat me. I was so terrified that I never again played in the fields—in fact, we were forbidden to go up the mountainside after this incident.

A good feature of this hot spring was that everyone bathed together. Beggars and aristocrats bathed side by side, and even though the sacred waters were shared by bathers with diseases and those without, nobody ever got infected. Since women bathed at a different time from the men, and the monks also bathed separately, there were no great concerns about privacy. In Lhasa during the summertime, everyone was together at the river, bathing and swimming. The men would be on one side, the women on the other. If they were too close together, the women would use large umbrellas: the umbrella would be held up by a servant or a female relative or friend, and the woman would bathe behind it, screened from view.

I never saw anyone naked. Women wore large cloths or towels to go to and from the river, and a *chobray*—a loose-fitting skirtlike garment—while in the water, as well as covering themselves with a towel. But there were always some women, wilder, louder, and less modest than the others, who weren't so concerned about being covered. After drinking chang—no doubt a bit too much—they would enter the river laughing and joking, wearing just a skirt with nothing on top.

The Lhasa Kyichu River (Lhasa's "joyous water") was not only too cold to bathe in, it was unsafe because it was very swift; so we used to bathe in a stream that flowed off it. There were some parts of the river that were extremely dangerous, as there were hidden whirlpools that could pull you down. A relative of mine drowned at one of these spots, along with an elderly family servant who jumped in to save him. Everyone stood by helplessly as they disappeared under the water. Sometime later, their bodies reappeared, rising up out of the whirlpool with the servant still holding tightly to his master, before they were pulled down again forever.

In Nyemo, there was a very nice river where you could bathe in the winter. Along the bank there were some places where you could dig down and the hole would fill up with hot water from an underground spring. We used to dig one of these holes, then put a tent over the hot pool and bathe. You could only do it in the winter because in the summer the river was much wider—too wide even for horses to cross. Sometimes the water was so hot that it burned our feet, so we left a wall of sand between the river and the hot pool, and when it was too hot we would open a small hole in the wall and channel some cold river water in. It was fun—we would go to the pool in a large group and have a party, and everyone enjoyed themselves tremendously.

CRAB APPLES

RINCHEN KHANDO CHOEGYAL

For a long time I was my parents' only child, and, because of all the attention I received, I became quite bold and independent. I was not the kind of person who liked to be waited on or served, although I always had to have someone accompanying me. I used to say to the servants, "You sit. I am going to do it myself." For instance, I wanted to look after my own clothes. I used to pick up my own laundry and take it indoors before it was dry. The next day, when I went to wear the clothes, they would still be damp. My mother would ask the servants who was responsible. The servants, who had been unable to stop me, would tell my mother that, as usual, I was responsible.

Where I lived in Kham there was a monastery that belonged to our family and that we had sponsored for many generations. It was a small monastery, much smaller than those of Lhasa. My uncle lived there with the other monks. Since it was only forty minutes away by horseback, I was able to visit easily. I was drawn to the monastery by my uncle's pet monkey and by a crab apple tree. One day, I was climbing this tree, which is what I invariably did when visiting, and my uncle shouted at me, "Whenever you come here you disturb my meditation. You make me feel that you are about to fall down and hurt yourself." I replied, "That is your fault. Who told you to disturb your meditation? If I fall I will be the one who will be hurt, not you. Either assign someone to pick these apples for me or let me pick them myself." He went back inside the monastery.

BONE EATER VULTURES

ZASEP TULKU RINPOCHE

Once my brother and I decided we would try to catch vultures. We had chosen to catch a large vulture known as the "bone eater"; this type is yellow and very large. It swallows and eats bones, hence its name. In Tibet it is called a *gho,* and elsewhere it is known as a lammergeier. One day, when I was around five years old, my brother and I saw that an animal had just died, and we knew that it would not be long before the vultures arrived. We took a rope and looped it over the corpse of the yak and then we hid behind a nearby boulder. The scavengers soon came. My brother and I watched, and, when we saw our chance, we pulled hard on the rope and succeeded in looping it around the neck of a large vulture. We kept pulling, but the vulture started to move down the side of the hill, trying to take off. We hung on to the rope, but the vulture was so strong that it dragged us along until I couldn't hang on anymore. My brother still kept a firm hold as the vulture kept dragging him further down the hill. I was scared that the bird was going to take off with him. Finally I saw my brother let go. That big bone eater, with the rope still hanging around its neck, just continued to fly off across the valley.

GIRL WATERING PLANTS IN A FARMHOUSE COURTYARD, VILLAGE EAST OF TAM'ALUNG, SHORE OF LAKE YAMDROK, TIBET

BOY PLAYING WITH A DONKEY DURING THE HARVEST, KORZAK VILLAGE, LAKE TSO MORARI, LADAKH, INDIA

YAK STRAINING ON HIS NOSE RING, LABRANG MONASTERY, AMDO PROVINCE, TIBET

GORED BY A YAK

JAMYANG SAKYA

I was gored quite badly by a yak when I was a child. You see, my family had a large number of yaks, and in the summertime we traveled with the herds for almost three months, living in tents. During this time, the whole family had to help make butter and cheese for the rest of the year. We were constantly around the yaks as well as the dri—the female yaks—and their young, so I got to know them very well. I knew them all individually, and even if there were a couple of hundred yaks together I could tell them apart. But show me three donkeys, and they all look the same to me! We children had to take care of the baby yaks while their mothers—the dri—were grazing. After a few hours, the dri would be brought home and we would have to do the milking. But first we would have to bring each dri her baby and show it to her, otherwise she wouldn't give any milk. I knew the animals so well that I could easily tell which baby belonged to which dri.

Two of our older yaks were used for ploughing the fields in the springtime. They had rings in their noses and, since they weren't used for riding, they still had their horns. They were very gentle animals and I used to play with them all the time, pulling their beautiful hair, their tails, their horns—they never seemed to mind. One day they brought the yaks to town to do the plowing. I was six or seven at the time. My aunt and I were responsible for bringing food to the plowmen and the yaks, so we came at lunchtime and fed the yaks while the workers ate the tsampa and yogurt that my aunt had prepared. While everyone was resting, I played with one of the yaks. As usual, I pulled his hair and tail and then, taking handfuls of grass, I started pushing the grass in his mouth and pulling it out again—just like I had so many times before. This time, the yak didn't seem too happy about it, but since he had always been so gentle I thought it was OK. So I yanked his horns hard, and that was when it happened.

The yak gored me in the face and threw me several feet in the air. My aunt ran over, crying out that I was dead. I was really scared. The yak's horn had gored me right through my cheek, and blood was everywhere. People gathered round, many of them weeping—such a commotion! They carried me at once to the nearby monastery and fetched my uncle, who was a doctor there. On the way my wounds were bleeding so badly that everyone kept saying, "She's finished," and I thought I was going to die! But my uncle looked after me. He was very wise, you know—the townspeople kept saying to him that the yak was bad and must be slaughtered, but he refused and said that they had to cut its horns and let it run wild. So the yak got its freedom—we "gave it to the Buddha," as we say. In fact, we used to give many yaks to the Buddha after they had done a certain amount of work. Once a year, everyone gathered at the monastery, and we would hang lots of prayer flags and put colorful banners on the yaks and let them go. After they are released their hair grows really long and they look beautiful. So after all those years of hard work the yak that gored me gained its freedom.

FARMING VILLAGE AND FIELDS DURING HARVEST, KORZAK VILLAGE, LAKE TSO MORARI, LADAKH, INDIA

ARISTOCRAT FARMER

SONAM DIKYI

The year the Chinese army arrived in Kham, my husband, who was a high-ranking official in the Tibetan government—a *tsepon*—was sent as a military officer to fight the Chinese. I was nineteen and we had only been married for six months. Ours was an arranged marriage, as was the custom. My family was aristocratic and very wealthy and my husband's family, although not very rich, was also of high status—his father was the prime minister of Tibet. I had known my husband by sight because we had gone to the same school, but when I was told of the arranged marriage, I had no particular feeling one way or the other.

I received most of my education from my father and only went to school between the ages of nine and twelve. Until then I had servants to look after me. Each day they would pack some food and take me to the gardens of the family estate, where we would spend the whole day playing, until it was time to come home in the evening. I had little interest in seeing my parents in the daytime—my first thought upon opening my eyes in the morning was to go outside and play. The estate was immense, with fields, forests, and lots of parks and gardens. Some of our land was rented out to other families, either because we didn't have the time to manage it all or because there weren't enough workers. Our main source of income was butter and grain, of which we produced huge amounts—in one day we could gather a thousand sacks of grain from the fields. These fields were divided up and each one given a name, which was recorded in a book. The largest one was called Chungde Chenmo, which means something like "Big Nature"; for each sack of seed that was planted, this field would produce twenty sacks of grain. While the fields were tended by our servants, nomads cared for our yaks and sheep up in the hills and mountains beyond the estate.

We had about thirty servants in our household. Some of them looked after the horses and mules, others made clothes, while still others wove carpets or *nambu*, the fabric from which the clothes were made. As well as the servants who worked in the fields, there were storekeepers, house cleaners, laundry workers, servants who looked after the children, and servants whose job it was to care for the elderly family members. There were even three servants whose only responsibility was to make chang every day. The servants mostly drank chang rather than tea; those with the most responsibility got large mugs of this drink while the others were served less. There was a limit on how much the servants were allowed to drink except on special days, when they were allowed to get a little drunk. To make the chang, cow dung was used for fuel, not wood, because cow dung produces just the right amount of heat, whereas wood is too hot and burns the chang before it can finish cooking.

When we children were older, about fifteen or sixteen, we went out to the fields with our parents to oversee the servants and make sure they did their jobs properly. The autumn was an important time because of the harvest, and our parents advised us to be alert and attentive to everything that was going on. If the weather was very hot, the grain would dry out and fall off the plant, and after the plants were cut the workers were supposed to pick up the fallen grain; we had to make sure that they did. Sometimes they would try to take advantage of our youthful kindheartedness, pleading with us not to make them pick up the grain because they were too tired. But then we would be very tough with them, for fear of what our parents would say. I had three brothers and three sisters. There was no difference between the boys and the girls; we all had the same responsibilities, although some of us were stricter than

FARMER MAKING CHANG, MINDO VILLAGE, NEAR GYATSA, TIBET

others. In fact, one of my brothers was mild and gentle like myself, while one sister was so ferocious that the servants were quite scared of her.

Every morning we would provide food for our servants. It was my job to beat the large wooden drum that summoned them to eat at eight o'clock every morning, by which time they were supposed to have finished their early work: milking the cows, churning butter, making chang—all had to be done by eight. The drum could be heard a long way away, and it was not only the servants who knew what it meant. Many poor families lived outside our property, and when they heard the drum they would come and ask us for food, which we always gave to them. Sometimes these people would bring gifts or offerings, such as vegetables, but even if they brought nothing they still received food.

After the drum was beaten to tell the servants it was time to come and eat, the supplies were made ready. Each servant got an equal measure of tsampa, which it was my job to serve. Tea and butter, being more expensive, were given out by my mother. The only time I can remember being disciplined by my mother was when I was about seventeen, after I gave some of the servants four ladles of apricots from our stores. They kept pressing me for them, and I didn't see anything wrong with giving them a few. When my mother learned of this, however, she was very upset that I had done it without asking her, and she got very angry with me.

During harvest time we would get up at three and leave the house around sunrise, taking tea and breakfast with us. It was quite cold, so we had to dress warmly. We always wore good clothes since we didn't have to do any physical work, whereas the servants normally wore goat or sheep skins, which hung down over the body, with a hole in the middle for the head to go through. There were always three servants in our house busy weaving the nambu cloth. The nambu that was woven into winter clothes was heavy and rough, while that used for summer clothes was lighter and softer.

We dressed for the day's work by ourselves, without the help of servants, but on special occasions we would need help with our jewelry and hair. It was customary to hire women to help with the braiding of hair and the special arrangements of jewelry that were necessary on such occasions. These women made their living this way, so they had no other work to do in our house and had lots of free time to chat and drink tea. My mother's hair and hat arrangement could be very complicated, and even with the help of these hired women it would take half a day to do. It was never necessary to spend this much time on my own hair.

Even my husband had to wear a certain hairstyle customary for high officials. Again, special people were hired to come and do this for him. It had to be done up in a formal style that was very complicated: after the hair was arranged on top of his head, a golden thunderbolt symbol or *vajra* was added. When he relaxed at home at the end of the day he would undo his hair and let it hang down, unless he was to meet with his father that evening. If so, he could not let his hair hang loose—it would have been improper to appear this way. He also had to wear official dress, without which he could not attend official functions. A very strict timetable was observed for seasonal changes of clothes: officials had to wear summer clothing until the day of the Great Prayer Festival, when they changed into their winter dress. This was worn for three months until the day of the Tibetan New Year, when summer dress was put on again.

For me, all this seemed quite natural. Women, too, were expected to dress and wear their hair according to custom, and never to be separated from their aprons or earrings. It was believed that the Dalai Lama's life-span would be shortened if the conventions of proper dress were abandoned, and that a man could develop obstacles in his spiritual progress if his wife were sloppy in these habits. When I washed my Tibetan apron, I never let it hang down when shaking out the water, but always held it face up as I flapped the water out. Again, if this were done improperly, difficulties might come to His Holiness or to family members. My grandmother was very strict about these things, and because of her presence

FARMHOUSE COURTYARD, EAST OF TAMALUNG, LAKE YAMDROK, TIBET

HORSES CORRALLED IN MONASTERY RUINS, TSURPHU MONASTERY,

DROWOLUNG VALLEY, TIBET

and the fact that this was a very strong tradition in Tibet, I never made a mistake in my dress. These habits were so ingrained that even when washing my hair I would never take off my apron, and if I had to take it off I never went so much as three steps away from it.

Life at home was very disciplined, in accordance with tradition and custom. For example, on winter evenings when everyone gathered in the main hall, the senior family members, particularly my parents, sat on raised seats so that they were sitting higher than the others. When we children were small, we ran everywhere and sat wherever we wanted, but when we were older we had our own seats below those of our parents, while the servants sat even lower. If my mother or father got up to leave the room, then out of respect all the children would stand as they left, and stand again when they returned. Naturally all the servants had to stand as well. Showing respect in this way was an everyday thing that we took for granted.

Our house was very old and had been the family home for many generations. An enormously heavy gate on the east side, and another on the west side, led into an open area where there were two storerooms at ground level, one for chang and the other for wool. The house had four stories. On the ground floor we stored hay for the animals, as well as the harvested barley and wheat. Two big steps on the north side of the house led up to two large mani wheels, which were in motion day and night, with two servants or villagers turning them continuously.

Past the mani wheels was the entrance to the second floor, where there was the first of our six shrine and altar rooms. This one was dedicated to Palden Lhamo, the protector goddess of Tibet, and here also there were always two monks doing prayers and offerings for us. Next to the shrine room was a three-pillar room (in Tibet we refer to the size of a room by the number of pillars needed to support the roof). This room was normally empty except in winter, when for ten days it would be used by sixty monks who were sent from the nearby monastery to say prayers for us.

Also on the second floor were our two meat storerooms. We never killed any animals and always traded barley to get our meat. In the fall we would trade with nomads, and by the end of October these rooms were filled with the dried meat of forty sheep and thirty yaks, all hanging from the ceiling. In a larger twelve-pillar room were kept the different types of tsampa and a type of pea that was grown as food for the horses. Nearby was a small two-pillar room for oil, which was stored in twenty big drums made of wood and yak skin, each drum holding thirty to forty buckets of oil. There were two more small rooms on this floor, one for making chang and the other for storing wool, and there was also a toilet.

The third floor was reached by going through a small gate near the mani wheels and then up some stairs. On this floor was the main shrine room—a twelve-pillar hall with many Buddha statues, a life-size statue of Tsong Khapa, and all the major texts and scriptures. Thangkas lined the walls, and on special days new thangkas would be displayed. Five monks from the neighboring monastery were always there, day and night, doing rituals and prayers. They lived with us for two months, after which they returned to the monastery and another five would be sent. This floor also held a room for the statue of our family's protector deity, rooms for the old people, a cooking room, a two-pillar common room where everyone gathered to eat, and the sleeping rooms. Young children slept with their mothers until they were about six, when they were moved to a special children's sleeping room, where servants slept with them in case they had to get up in the night.

The center of the house was an open courtyard on the third floor where grass and other grains could be stored, and the roof was the fourth floor that was built around it, with glass on three sides and a wall on the fourth. There were a few rooms on this top floor: a one-pillar room with an altar and a life-size clay statue to which we made offerings for good fortune, a shrine room with two pillars, and another two-pillar room for entertaining visitors. This room was usually used for storing

WINNOWING BARLEY, THIKSE MONASTERY, LADAKH, INDIA

SEPARATING GRAIN FROM CHAFF, THIKSE MONASTERY, LADAKH, INDIA

cushions, but when we had festivals such as Losar (Tibetan New Year), when many people would come to the house, we would take them to this room and bring out mats for them to sit on. The rest of the roof was empty, and people could go there to sit in the sun.

In the evenings we would gather together in the main hall—mainly the women, as the men would be off visiting friends—and the female servants would work with wool, carding, spinning, and making clothes. During these times, I liked to knit, but this was not a duty—I did it for pleasure. If it was winter, we would sit around the fireplace and do our work by the light that came from tall, rounded oil lamps that burned with an open flame. Like most of our utensils the lamps were made of clay, though sometimes of metal. My parents usually did their evening prayers, sometimes talking to each other, and we would all sit together until it was time for sleep at around eleven o'clock. My parents rose at about three or four A.M. to do their morning prayers before they started the day. The servants would rise at about five, and we children, because we were young and needed more sleep, around seven. In the springtime we would all rise earlier, as this was a busy time of year—everyone knew that the more work we did in the spring, the better things would go at harvest time.

At certain times of the year it was the custom for us to give specific gifts. For example, every year we would give each of our servants a set of winter clothes and summer clothes. At Tibetan New Year and on all religious festivals they would be given special foods. Our servants were not paid a wage, but each person or family would be given a field, large or small, and animals, depending on the size of their family and their needs. In return they would choose one family member to be our servant. Two or three family members were expected to spend some time each day working on our fields, but the rest of the time they looked after their own affairs.

There was a particular time in the winter when people from our house would go to the monastery, to make offerings on three successive days. I was usually the one in charge of this, and on each of the three days I would arrive at the monastery with some servants and about ten mules or horses loaded with our offerings. There were about a hundred monks, and each day each one of them would receive about five kilograms of butter, five bags of khapse—a sort of Tibetan cookie—and a bag of tsampa. The senior lamas received maybe a little bit extra. If we had had a good season we could offer more; if not, there would be less. After making the offering to the monks we returned home. On the following day we made the same journey with the same offerings, and again on the third day.

During the year we would sometimes ask the monastery to send monks to our house to perform religious services. On these occasions our offerings to them would be more elaborate—butter, cheese, and dried meat. Some of the monks in this monastery were very poor, and they would come to our house to ask us for food; we never let them leave empty-handed. A few of them made incense to sell, and they would ask us to buy it. There were also two nunneries in the area, which we supported, often making offerings of money for them to do special pujas for us.

When the Chinese came, we were ordered to abandon many of our customs and beliefs. But I had a very strong faith in all our traditions and always followed them, and I think that this has brought good results. After the invasion, my husband and I decided we would face whatever came to us. My husband spent twenty years in prison in Tibet: this is the way things happen in life. But I feel happy and content. I can still see His Holiness the Dalai Lama here in Dharamsala, and I feel that without my strong beliefs in our traditions I might have died in Tibet.

FIELD OF MUSTARD, NEAR TSETHANG, TIBET

NOMAD TENT AND STORM CLOUD, ZOROUG CHU VALLEY, TIBET

CONTROLLING WEATHER

KARMA LHUNDUP, SHOPA LAMA

For many generations my family's job was to protect crops from all forms of destruction by natural forces. My father came to me when I was twenty-two years old and told me that he was entering a meditation retreat in the mountains and that it was now my duty to take over his role. I was worried when I first attempted to control the weather and was afraid that all the crops would be destroyed, but after two or three years I came to trust my vocation.

I practiced at a monastery where there were eight other *nagpas*, shamans who performed rituals. We were supported by the Tibetan government with money and food, and each of us was designated a "controller of weather" and given an official government stamp. At the start of each planting year we held many retreats in which prayers and rituals were performed to Vajrakilaya. Afterwards, all around the areas to be protected, wooden *phurba*s, or ritual thunderbolt daggers, were placed in the ground. The area for which I was responsible was large, and it took many, many days to put these daggers in the ground. During this process all the farmers would participate by performing ritual ceremonies. Since we took great care to fulfill all the requirements, we were successful each year in protecting the crops.

As a weather controller I had responsibilities throughout the year. Much of my time was spent in a three-story red house; this was a special building, constructed solely for my use by the people of our region. The red house was built in the very center of the fields I was to protect; from there I could see any clouds approaching. It is well known that,

through the study of cloud movements, it is possible to determine the kind of weather that is approaching; what is not well known, and what I cannot reveal, are those skills and practices through which clouds can be moved away.

I would enter the red house just before the seeds began to appear on the plant and I would stay there, throughout the harvest, until the fields had been completely cleared of the crops. Though my residence was a form of retreat, I had a servant who saw to my needs and I received many visitors. At times there were requests to protect regions outside my area and I was able to comply with these requests also without leaving. On occasion, people would come to make incense offerings. People also came and asked me to do divinations—especially in the event of sickness, when they would want to know which doctor to visit. In fact, until the Chinese arrived, I was kept very busy.

I stopped hailstorms for twenty-two years, until I was forty-four, and on no occasion did hail fall on those fields for which I was responsible. There are nagpas who possess the skills necessary to bring rain, but my practice only permits me to stop hailstorms. In fact we never needed rainmakers in our region because the rains always came on time. I escaped the Chinese military when they invaded Tibet, only to learn later that my father had been caught and had died in prison. The crops remained safe for one year, but then the red house was competely destroyed by the invading armies. In the following year, hailstones fell throughout our region and the crops were completely destroyed.

NOMAD YOGI, SUMED TIBETAN NOMAD CAMP, LADAKH, INDIA

MONKS AND BUTTER LAMPS, RAMOCHE MONASTERY, LHASA, TIBET

RETURN FROM THE DEAD

CHAGDUD TULKU

There were several highly realized lamas in each generation of the Tromge family, and my mother, Dawa Drolma, was the most famous in hers. She was one of Tibet's five great wisdom *dakinis*—female emanations who spontaneously benefit other sentient beings by their activities. It had been prophesied that she would be born as an emanation of the longevity deity White Tara, an incarnation of Tibet's most revered female practitioner and the spiritual companion of Padmasambhava, the master who propagated Buddhist teachings in Tibet in the eighth century. Dawa Drolma was also a *delog*, one who has crossed the threshold of death and traveled in realms of existence beyond those visible to humans and returned to tell about it.

One day, when my mother was about sixteen, the goddess Tara appeared to her, not in a luminous vision but in person. Tara told my mother that she would soon fall ill and die, but if she followed certain instructions explicitly, she would be able to revivify her dead body and benefit others by teaching about her experience. Soon after, Dawa Drolma had a series of bad dreams about three demonic sisters who were robbing all beings of their vitality. With black lariats and silk banners they tried to ensnare Dawa Drolma around the waist, but the deity White Tara prevented them from doing so by surrounding her with a protection circle. Eventually, however, the menace in the dreams was so strong that Dawa Drolma knew it foretold her imminent death. She went to her uncle, the great Tromge Trungpa Rinpoche, and with his help made the necessary arrangements for her death, just as Tara had instructed. Then she became extremely sick and died, despite the efforts of the many doctors who were summoned to care for her.

Exactly as she had stipulated prior to her death, Dawa Drolma's corpse was washed in consecrated saffron water and dressed in new clothes. The corpse was carefully laid out in a room and left without a morsel of food or a drop of water. The door was draped in blue cloth, padlocked, and sealed with the sign of the wrathful fire scorpion. A man dressed in blue stood guard outside. All the local people were warned to refrain from ordinary chatter, and they were instructed to recite prayers and mantras. For the next five days and nights Tromge Trungpa, along with several other lamas and monks, did prayers and ceremonies in the adjacent room. At the completion of this vigil, Tromge Trungpa entered the room where the corpse lay, cold and pale just as he had left it, and he recited powerful long-life prayers to summon Dawa Dolma's mindstream back into her body. In the account she dictated several days after her return, she described her reentry into her body:

When the consciousness reentered my physical body, I sneezed violently and experienced total disorientation. An instant later, I was in a state of faith and joy at the visions of the pure realm, and horror at the karmic visions of hell. I felt as though I were waking up from sleep. Uncle Trungpa was standing in front of me, holding a longevity arrow and looking at me with concern in his bloodshot eyes. I was unable to say a word, as though I were a bit shy. Everyone was crying and excited, and saying things such as, "Wasn't it difficult?" "You must be hungry!" "You must be thirsty!" They were almost pouring food and drink over my head. Although I protested, saying, "I feel absolutely no discomfort due to hunger or thirst," they didn't believe me.

Everyone was saying, "Eat! Drink!" They all felt joy as immeasurable as a she-camel who has found her lost calf. We all partook of a feast to celebrate.

During her five-day journey as a delog, my mother's consciousness, unhindered by the constraints of a physical body, traveled freely through all the realms of mind, from the hell realms with their ceaseless, unbearable suffering to the most exalted pure lands of the wisdom beings. For the rest of her life, whenever my mother taught, she drew from her experience as a delog. Her descriptions of the misery of the other realms were very vivid, and tears came to her eyes as she spoke. "No matter how difficult your life is in this human realm," she would say, "there is no comparison between the difficulties here and those in other realms." No one doubted that she spoke from direct experience, and her credibility was enhanced by the messages she brought to people from their deceased relatives.

MAGICAL SEEDS

TSERING DOLKAR YUTHOK

There was a very tall and thin woman, originally from Kham, who lived near us. Her family told us that when she slept her body was so cold it was as if she were dead. She had magical powers; people saw her obtain ordinary objects right out of thin air. At other times she would tell stories of events she had foreseen. In one dream she saw the Chinese invading, dressed in yellow uniforms, and later the invasion happened just as she had dreamed it. Over time, people came to believe that she was not an ordinary human and that perhaps she was even some sort of heavenly being or dakini.

One season her family had a serious shortage of seed grain. The family was discussing what to do—whether to borrow or buy it—and they asked the woman from Kham to help. She told them not to be concerned and asked all the family members to stay together in one room that night, instead of sleeping in their own beds. During the night strange things happened. Noises could be heard from the empty storeroom, and, after some time, everyone heard the sound of pouring grain. The next day they went to the storeroom and found it full of barley.

VISION DANCE

JAMPA LHUNDUP

When I was nine, I went to Ratö Monastery near Lhasa to become a monk. After several years there I became very interested in singing songs, especially a certain type of song and dance popular in Kham called Tö. Tö is a kind of musical verse composed by very high lamas. The movements to the accompanying dance are slow and elegant. I was mesmerized by each performance I saw, and soon I became almost desperate to learn it.

Although Tö is spiritual and has religious words, monks are not allowed to study such songs and dances. They are granted permission to sing and dance Tö just once a year, at Losar, during the traditional New Year's picnic. Since my religious studies were my main occupation, I had to learn the song secretly. Whenever I had some free time, such as on holidays, I would travel to a quiet, faraway place to study.

When I was learning the song and dance I was caught several times and summoned back to the monastery, where I was punished and told to stop learning the Tö. As you can imagine, I felt very sad; I didn't know what I would do if I could not learn this song. I continued my secret studies until my teacher died, by which time I had managed to learn almost all of the song's text.

My teacher came from my region in Kham and, although he was not a monk, he had studied with a lama named Tonguoso Rinpoche, who wrote down the words to the *Tö*. Tonguoso Rinpoche received the complete text in a vision. It is said that this vision occurred in the Tibetan Year of the Water Bird, during the reign of the Thirteenth Dalai Lama. At that time a war was raging in Tibet. The lama taught the Tö to the local people, including my teacher, requesting that his students spread the knowledge of it to all the people of the Dhakyap region. It was believed that if the song and dance could be spread, then the war would end. When the

lama died, however, the Tö had hardly been taught anywhere beyond the tiny area from which he came, and so the war continued. Then, the Chinese came to Dhakyap and burned the houses and killed many people. Much destruction took place, except in the small area where the lama had lived and taught the Tö. This magic song and dance would surely have saved the whole of Dhakyap if only the knowledge of it had been spread further.

The dance is performed differently in various parts of Tibet. In central Tibet dancers wear special costumes and use drums. In Kham, however, dancers wear chubas, big metal amulets on their chests, and swords at their sides. Long ago, performers wore a kind of raw silk wrapped around their heads, but later this was replaced by fur hats. Today, dancers braid their hair with various ornaments, rings, and other decorative items.

The Tö can be performed for a half a day or all day, depending on the number of parts included. In the text written down by Tonguoso Rinpoche there are one hundred and seventy chapters and parts for thirty to forty dancers. Each chapter of the song has different words, tunes, and styles of dance. No matter what the final length of the dance, the first three sections are always performed. After that it is up to the dance leader to decide how much more to perform.

The first part of the Tö is an offering to the various Buddhist deities. The second part appeases the local spirits that inhabit the land where the Tö is being performed, so that when the dancers make a noise the spirits are not disturbed. The third part summons the crowd; it is an invitation and announcement to the people to come and witness the performance. Subsequent parts of the Tö describe rivers, sacred mountains, villages, monasteries, and so on.

MASKED DANCERS, TSURPHU MONASTERY, TIBET

MONKS DRESSED AS SNOW LIONS PREPARING FOR A SACRED DANCE, TSURPHU MONASTERY, TIBET

Practicing Dance Steps, Mindroling Monastery, Tibet

After coming to India, I lost touch with this tradition and now I have forgotten many of the verses. The full text no longer exists, although I have written down all the verses I can remember. I have heard that performances of the Tö have started again in the Dhakyap region, but they are not that pure.

Perhaps the reason I persisted in learning the Tö, despite being told time and again to stop doing so, is because the words and music are so beautiful and sacred. Good fortune and success will come to those who recite the text of this magical song.

THE OPERA SINGER
NORBU TSERING

I was a very beautiful child and also very good at singing opera, which was quite natural since my parents were opera singers. When I was eight years old I began performing. When a song is sung by a child in Tibetan opera, it is customary for the song to begin with the word *liee,* which is sung in a swelling, high-pitched tone. I think I must have mispronounced this word, because I was nicknamed "Laba," which is derived from *liee,* and I have been known by that name ever since.

For my first appearance in opera, I played Padmasambhava as a child, sitting in a lotus flower. I sang one song, then my father walked onstage in front of the audience, picked me up, and carried me off. When I was nine, I joined the opera troupe and began my training, studying throughout the year, even when there were no performances. Voice training took place very early in the morning beside a local waterfall. Standing between a large rock and the falls, we shouted out our scales and listened to our voices echoing back. After a while with this kind of training the voice grows much stronger, louder even than the sound of the waterfall. Today, we still send our students to the local waterfall to develop the power of their voices.

We were given opera parts according to our age and the way we looked, and so of course our roles changed as we grew older. A mask was used if there was no suitable person available to play a certain part. For example, if there was a character in the opera who was a very old man and there was no actor old enough to play him, then a young person might play the part by wearing a mask. He would use movement and gesture to portray his character, whereas another character might be played by an actor without a mask who showed different moods and emotions through his facial expressions. It's very important for actors to learn all these different facial expressions.

There were twelve opera troupes in central Tibet, and I belonged to the most famous one, the Qumo Lomga, which had over one hundred members. On official occasions our troupe was required to perform at places like Norbulingka Palace, the Potala, and Drepung Monastery. Our women members were not allowed to perform in palaces and monasteries, so it was customary for the men to take their places. I often used to play female roles because I was very good-looking and could imitate a woman very well. By my gestures and the way I moved my body I was able to appear quite feminine, and I became very famous because of this. If I happened to go to the market in Lhasa in the evenings, everyone would joke with me about playing the part of a woman.

The girls, especially, teased me—particularly the daughters of wealthy families. They all liked to be around me because I was good-looking. They wrote me love letters, and there was even a popular song

Musicians on a Monsoon Morning, Namgyal Monastery, Dharamsala, India

composed about me. The song refers to the time that I and other members of the troupe were sent to India by the government to learn a certain style of dance. We had used the dance in an opera scene with a Moghul king, after some members who had previously visited India showed us how to do it. People liked it so much that the government sent us to India to learn the dance style. So then this song became popular:

Laba was sent to India on government orders,
But the girls do not cry
Because it would bring sadness to Laba's life.

During the Shoten Festival, which dates back to the fifteenth century, many troupes came to Lhasa to perform. Opera singers are paid to perform, and during the festival a particular lama institute called Kundeling was responsible for paying our troupe. Afterwards, the other troupes returned to their own region, but we remained in Lhasa, although at other times we also had to travel to different areas to perform and practice. We traveled over long distances, to places as far away as Kongpo and Lhoka, using horses, donkeys, and mules to carry all our costumes and equipment. When we arrived, we would be given many privileges, such as inexpensive housing.

While we were traveling, the members of the troupe who had managed to save a little money did some business on the side. Since I was very famous and a favorite of the aristocratic families, I received many gifts from them and I didn't really need to do business. I didn't have to leave Lhasa very often, either. However, some of the families took me with them when they went to trade fairs in Lhoka. I spent a lot of time going to fairs. I would often go to Jampaling Monastery for a seven-day fair, traveling down the Tsangpo River in a yak-skin boat called a *cowa*.

Although I didn't do much business, there were times when my wealthy friends gave or lent me money so that I could buy imported textiles and cigarettes for trading on these trips. Most often I traded them for a special textile from Lhoka. This area is noted for a heavy woolen fabric called *nambu*, which is used for making chubas. Weavers use wool from different parts of the sheep to make different types of this material. For example, wool taken from the belly of the sheep is very soft, but the softest, finest-quality nambu is made with wool from the sheep's testicles. This material is so fine that a big piece of it can easily be rolled up and slipped through a finger ring.

As I grew older, my parts in the opera changed. My looks had faded, you see, and I could no longer play the role of a young woman. So then I became responsible for training the person who was to take my place. Also, people used to come to me and ask me to teach them to sing. In Tibet, everyone knew bits of opera songs—it was a very popular form of music. Within the aristocratic families there were people who really knew the art well, and in fact some could sing opera songs better than the professional performers.

For several years, I spent most of my time with the aristocracy and it was a very happy time for me. Later, when I had grown older and was no longer popular, life was much harder, as I had to travel with the troupe to other parts of Tibet to perform and practice. But I have experienced life at all levels of society—with the very rich, with the very poor, and finally with my peers.

REMAINS OF AN OLD FRESCO, THIKSE MONASTERY, LADAKH, INDIA

EVERYTHING MUST GO

ZASEP TULKU RINPOCHE

Six months before the Chinese invaded Lhasa, a lama from Sakya Monastery said that he wanted to do a big fire puja, a ritual fire in which offerings are burned for the purpose of purification. He told everyone to buy all different types of grain and seeds, such as barley, rice, black sesame seed, and so on. The people thought, "Well, for a big fire puja we'll need a lot," so they obtained a great quantity of each type of grain and seed. The day of the fire puja came, and the first thing the lama said to his wife was that she should bring all her jewelry to him. When she asked him, "What are you going to do?" he said, "I'm going to do a fire puja." She was really worried. "Those are my precious turquoise, corals, and *dzi*s," she said in a shocked voice. He said, "No, no. I'm really serious." She wasn't happy but . . . he was the lama. She brought all the jewels and he threw them into the fire. Then he threw some of his own possessions on the fire, including some ritual objects and Buddhist texts. He told his students, "Whatever you want to bring, just throw it in. Throw everything into the fire." So it was no longer an ordinary fire puja. Strange things were burning and the smells were completely different from those to which everyone was accustomed. Then he told the whole monastery, "Bring all the decorations from inside the monastery, those banners and the long brocades, everything, and throw them into the fire." Some people were certain that the lama had gone mad.

Six months later the Chinese invaded; during the Cultural Revolution everything was destroyed. Then everyone at Sakya Monastery understood the lama and his strange fire puja.

MONKS LOOKING OUT INTO A MONASTERY COURTYARD, TRANDRUK MONASTERY, TIBET

FIERCE AND UNCOMPROMISING ASPECT OF TRUTH SYMBOLIZED
BY A TIGER SKIN, DOOR AT LAMALING MONASTERY, TIBET

IMPERMANENCE SYMBOLIZED BY A FLAYED HUMAN SKIN,
DOOR AT LAMALING MONASTERY, TIBET

Chagdud Tulku was born in 1930 in Kham. His mother was well known as an accomplished practitioner. At the age of three he was recognized as a reincarnation of the previous Chagdud Tulku. While still young, he studied the Six Yogas of Naropa, and he completed a three-year retreat at age eleven. After his escape from Tibet, Chagdud Rinpoche worked in various refugee camps, making use of his medical knowledge and instructing people in powa practice. He has established teaching centers in Canada and the United States.

Choe Phuntsok was born in 1921 into a farming family at Namring in the province of Tsang. He is a master wood-carver and teacher at the Norbulingka Centre for Arts near Dharamsala, India.

Dakthdun Jampa Gyeltsen was born in Lhasa in 1939 into a family of government officials. In 1960 he escaped to Bhutan and in 1967 arrived in Dharamsala. He is currently the director of the Tibetan Institute of Medical and Astro Sciences.

Gekoe Lobsang Samdup was born at Lhoka Dranang and at the age of six entered Ganden Monastery and became a monk. During his many years in the monastery, he fulfilled a great number of tasks and positions. He is now retired and lives in Dharamsala.

Gelong Lobsang Dhonden was born in 1912 to the Tundra Mandronpa family. His father was a treasurer to the Tun family, and they lived on this family's large estate. He lived in the region called Nyemo, about two days' journey by foot west of Lhasa. After his wife died he became a monk in 1968 and now lives in Dharamsala.

Gyeten Namgyal was born in the Year of the Water Mouse, 1912. His father was a tailor, and master of robes, to a high-ranking lama. Gyeten Namgyal followed in his father's footsteps and became the personal tailor of two successive Dalai Lamas. Now in his eighties, Namgyal lives in Dharamsala.

Jampa Lhundup teaches at the Tibetan Institute of Performing Arts in Dharamsala. He was born in 1932 at Dakyap in Kham. His farming family occasionally made trading and business trips to Lhasa, and at the age of nine he entered monastic life in Lhasa at Ratö Monastery.

Jamyang Sakya was born into a family of moderate affluence in the region of eastern Tibet known as Kham. At a very early age she went on a pilgrimage with her family to Sakya. It was in Sakya that she met and became engaged to the present holder of the Sakya Khon lineage, H.H. Jigdal Dagchen Sakya Rinpoche. In 1960 she and her family emigrated to the United States, very shortly after escaping the occupying armies of the Chinese government. After great difficulty they established the Sakya Tegchen Choling Monastery, where Dagchen Rinpoche oversees a group of Sakya teaching centers.

Karma Lhundup, Shopa Lama, was born in 1916 in Dhoeshargar in western Tibet. His only education was in scripture and Buddhist practice; he first studied at Shari Mendzikang Monastery. Like his father, Nawang Tenzin Norbu, and many previous generations, Karma Lhundup was trained to be a nachang nagpa, or weather controller, with the ability to control hailstorms. From the age of seventeen to twenty-one he underwent strict religious retreats close to Mount Everest. At the age of twenty-two he became the head of his monastery.

Kayma Lhamo and her brother **Pema Thinley** were born into a nomadic family in the Ngari district of Tibet.

Kelsang Tashi was born into a nomadic family in the Ngari Rudok district of western Tibet. He was sixty years of age at the time of the interview in 1994. As a young man he was often called upon to capture and train the wild horses that his nomadic community required. He now lives in a Tibetan refugee settlement known as Choglamsar, near Leh, Ladakh, India.

Kunga Peljor was born in 1929 at Lharuko in Kham. His family was primarily nomadic, but had a small parcel of land for farming. He now lives in the Tibetan settlement of Choglamsar, Ladakh, India.

Lati Rinpoche Jangchub Tsultrim was born in the province of Kham in 1923. After being identified as an incarnate lama, he entered a local monastery called Dagyab. From the age of nine through fifteen he remained at Dagyab and then proceeded to Ganden Shartse Monastery near Lhasa. After fleeing the occupation of Tibet, Lati Rinpoche spent one year in the refugee camp at Buxaduar in West Bengal, and then fifteen years at Namgyal Monastery in Dharamsala, assisting in the religious affairs of the Dalai Lama. He was appointed abbot of Ganden Shartse Monastery in 1977 and held this position until 1984. He is currently the tutor to Trichang Rinpoche's reincarnation.

Lobsang Gyaltso was born in 1928 at Khunzerawa, in a region of Tibet close to the border of Burma. Neither wealthy nor poor, his family lived as semi-nomads. From the age of eleven to seventeen he studied as a monk at his village monastery and returned home on holidays to help with family work. Lobsang Gyaltso is the principal of the Institute of Buddhist Dialectics in Dharamsala.

Nagchang Yeshe Dorje Rinpoche was born in 1926 in the Markham region of Tibet and died in Dharamsala at the age of sixty-eight. At five years of age he was recognized as an incarnate lama and former abbot of Do-Nag Choling Monastery. Yeshe Dorje first made rain in his early thirties after a series of long retreats. Yeshe Dorje's accounts were told by his student Nagpa Karma Lhundup.

Ngawangthongdup Narkyid was born in 1931 in Staytong in the district of Naytong to a farming family. He entered school in 1942 in the Potala, finished in 1948, and immediately became a government clerk there. He lives in Dharamsala and is compiling an official biography of His Holiness the Dalai Lama.

Norbu Tsering was born in 1927 in Lhasa and began to perform as an opera singer at the age of eight. He is now an instructor at the Tibetan Institute of Performing Arts in Dharamsala.

Norgya the Nomad was born in Shagar in 1921 and currently lives in Dharamsala.

Pema Dorje came from a farming background and was born in the village of Tsetang in 1930. He is one of the very few Tibetan master metalworkers still living. Pema Dorje practices his craft and teaches at the Norbulingka Centre for Arts near Dharamsala.

Rinchen Khando Choegyal is the minister of education for the Central Tibetan administration of the Dalai Lama. Born in Dhargye Gompa, in the province of Kham, Tibet, Rinchen Khando escaped her homeland in 1959. She was active in the Tibetan Youth Congress and received her bachelor's degree at Loreto College in Darjeeling, India. She is married to the younger brother of the Dalai Lama and is the mother of a son and a daughter.

Rinzin Wangyal, at the time of the interview, in 1994, was seventy-one. Born at Rawang in the Rudhok district of Ngari, he lived a farming and nomadic life with his family. He lives in the Tibetan refugee settlement of Choglamsar, Ladakh, India.

Sonam Dikyi believes she was born in 1931. Her family was from the aristocratic level of Tibetan society and had a large farming estate in the Nyemo area. In 1949 she married into the Lhukhang family; at that time her father-in-law was the prime minister of Tibet. In 1991 she was ordained as a nun and now lives in Dharamsala.

Sonam Tsering was born in the Phempo region of Tibet and worked as a muleteer, or telpa, for his lama. Sonam was a noted horse racer and rode the celebrated Yonluk to victory in 1959, the year China invaded Tibet.

Geshe Tashi Namgyal was born in Sakya, Tibet, in 1922. At the age of eight he entered the Sakya Monastery of Thubten Llakhang Chenmo, took full monk's vows at twenty-one, and at age twenty-five obtained the Geshe Degree of Dungrbjampa. In 1960, after having been imprisoned by the Chinese occupation army, he fled to India and joined the Sakyaguru Monastery in Darjeeling, India. In 1972, at the request of the Dalai Lama, he volunteered to accompany a group of refugees to Canada as one of four spiritual leaders and now lives in Victoria, British Columbia.

Dr. Trogawa Rinpoche was born in 1932 in central Tibet. He was recognized as the reincarnation of the well-known medical lama Drag-lhoong Gomchen Paljor Gyaltsen. At the age of twelve he entered the Mindrol Rabten Ling Monastery; from the age of sixteen to twenty-four he studied Tibetan medicine as an apprentice to Dr. Narongshar in Lhasa. For the last ten years he has been working to establish the Chagpori Tibetan Medical Institute in Darjeeling.

Tsangpa Gyachen was born in 1916 at Gyerge in the Ngari region of western Tibet. His family shared their valley with three other nomadic families. A three-day journey by horse was required to circle their entire pasture land. He lives in the Tibetan refugee settlement of Choglamsar, Ladakh, India.

Tsering Dolkar Yuthok was born into the family of Sholkhang in 1923. Mrs. Yuthok's grandfather was the prime minister of Tibet during the Thirteenth Dalai Lama's incarnation. Her father was the chief treasurer of the Potala Palace and later became governor of Lhoka Province. Her husband, Mr. Yuthok, was appointed chief justice and thereafter cabinet minister in the Tibetan government. Mrs. Yuthok left Tibet in 1956 for a pilgrimage to India and was forced to remain when it became obvious that the Chinese occupation was going to completely engulf her country. Mrs. Yuthok now lives in Vancouver, British Columbia.

Tsewang Tashi was born into a nomadic trading family at Nachku, within the Sakya district, in 1926. He was imprisoned by the Chinese government in 1960 and then released in 1981. After escaping to India he came to Dharamsala and now lives in Tsechok Ling Monastery.

Dr. Yeshe Dhonden was born in 1929 into a wealthy family of farmers living in the small village of Namro. At the age of six he was accepted as a novice monk in the local monastery of Shedrup Ling. He studied in Lhasa and practiced medicine throughout Tibet until his escape into Bhutan in 1959. After leaving Tibet and serving in the refugee camps he became personal physician to the Dalai Lama.

Yeshi Jimpa started school at the age of nine and at fifteen entered a monastery, studying both at Potala Palace and Namgyal Monastery. He fled Tibet at the age of fifteen in 1959 and lived in India for twelve years. Yeshi and his wife have two daughters and live and work in Longueuil, Quebec.

Zasep Tulku Rinpoche, at the age of five, was installed as the abbot of Zuru Monastery in the Llarong Gedun Dorje Jungpug region of Nangchen Kham, having been recognized as the reincarnation of the previous abbot. After beginning his formal training at age seven, he traveled to Sera Je Monastery near Lhasa and continued his studies and practice after leaving Tibet due to the dangers of the Chinese occupation. Zasep Rinpoche has established the Ganden Choling and Zuru Ling centers in Canada.

arhat Buddhist saint; a follower of the Buddha who has attained freedom from ignorance and suffering.

blessing cords Small strings blessed by lamas and worn for protection against disease and ill fortune (in Tibetan, *sung du,* meaning "protection").

bodhisattva In Mahayana Buddhism, one who, having attained enlightenment (bodhi), is on his way to Buddhahood and postpones entering nirvana in order to keep a vow to help all sentient beings attain salvation.

Buddha An awakened One. Refers to Sakyamuni (Siddhartha Gautama), the Indian prince who became an All-Enlightened Being, the historic founder of Buddhism, and to others believed to be capable of assisting Buddhist believers.

butter lamp Lamp using melted butter; in Tibetan, *chome.*

chang Tibetan beer made from fermented barley or other grains.

Chenrezi Bodhisattva of Compassion; Tibetan manifestation of India's Avalokiteshvara.

chuba Traditional Tibetan dress; an ankle-length, wraparound garment worn by men and women.

circumambulation In Tibetan, called *kora;* the clockwise circling of religious shrines for acquisition of merit.

Dalai Lama Spiritual and temporal leader of Tibet, believed to be the emanation of Avalokiteshvara, or Chenrezi, the Bodhisattva of Compassion.

dakini Female spirit/angel who assists yogis in attaining miraculous states; in Tibetan, *khandro,* literally, "sky-goer."

dharma Sanskrit word used in Buddhism to mean the way, the law, the teachings of the Lord Buddha.

dob-dob Monk often occupied with discipline and physical labor in the monastery.

dri Female yak.

dzi Black-and-white–patterned onyx stone, highly prized in Tibet.

dzo Male offspring of a *dri* (female yak) and a domestic cattle animal. The *dzomo* is the female.

geshe Academic degree in the Gelugpa school of Buddhism, equivalent to a doctorate of Buddhist philosophy; a monk holding such a degree.

gompa Tibetan monastery or nunnery.

guru Religious teacher or leader.

gyanamani Huge wall of *mani* stones.

Jokhang Temple Temple in Lhasa housing the Jowo chempo, the statue of the Buddha that is Tibet's holiest object.

Jowo chempo Sacred gold statue of the Buddha housed in the Jokhang Temple, brought to Tibet as a present from the Chinese princess Wen Cheng when she came to marry King Songtsen Gampo in the seventh century.

Kalachakra Buddhist teaching and public empowerment initiation into mystical practice to ward off general difficulties.

Kham Eastern province of Tibet whose inhabitants are known as Khampas.

khata White ceremonial scarf used as an offering to sacred images and to venerated lamas, as well as a customary gift when greeting or bidding farewell to someone.

kora Circumambulation; the clockwise circling of religious shrines for acquisition of merit.

lama Tibetan spiritual teacher, master, or sage; literally, "none higher."

Losar: Tibetan New Year.

mani stone Smooth stone inscribed with the universal mantra "Om Mani Padme Hum"; placed in piles near temples and beside pilgrim paths.

mandala Sacred creation incorporating colors, symbols, graphic elements, and deities depicting the enlightened state of mind.

mantra Sanskrit term used in both Buddhism and Hinduism to signify a sacred syllable, word, or verse that embodies in sound some specific deity or supernatural power; literally, "protection of the mind."

Monlam Also known as Monlam Chenmo, this is the Great Prayer Festival, held in Lhasa just after the Tibetan New Year and instituted in the fifteenth century by Tsong Khapa. It is attended by monks from the monastic universities of Sera, Ganden, and Drepung. During the twenty-one-day ceremony the city magistrates had no power or discipline, and order in the city was kept by two chief monks from Drepung Monastery.

Mount Kailas Also known as Kang Rinpoche, 22,028 feet high, in western Tibet. It has been considered sacred by Buddhists, Hindus, Jains, and Bonpos for thousands of years. For Tibetan Buddhists it is an important place of pilgrimage, and thousands travel there to begin the sacred circumambulation along a thirty-four-mile path that climbs to 18,600 feet.

mudra One of a variety of hand gestures performed in specific tantric rituals; literally, "hand seal."

nagpa Shaman/priest employed to work spells and perform rituals.

nambu Woven cloth used for making clothes.

Norbulingka His Holiness the Dalai Lama's summer palace in Lhasa; literally, "Jewel Park."

Om Mani Padme Hum Mantra of the Bodhisattva of Compassion, Avalokiteshvara, which means "Hail to the Jewel in the Lotus."

Padmasambhava Also known as Guru Rinpoche, Padmasambhava was invited to come from India to Tibet in 747. There he exorcised demons by supernatural powers and founded the earliest Tibetan Buddhist sect.

Panchen Lama "Guru who is a great scholar." The Panchen Lama is revered as the emanation of the Buddha Amitabha and after the Dalai Lama is considered the second most important leader in Tibet.

phurba Ritual dagger with a three-sided blade, representing the liberation of the three mental poisons: anger, grasping, and stupidity.

Potala Palace Winter residence of the Dalai Lamas, built in the seventeenth century and containing over one thousand rooms. It was built on the Red Hill of Lhasa, the Tibetan capital, and rises more than 300 meters (1,000 feet) above the valley floor.

powa Transference of consciousness, particularly at the moment of death, into states of higher consciousness.

prayer flags Squares of cotton cloth in five colors with prayers or mantras printed by woodblock. Prayer flags are hung in clusters on roofs, in mountain passes, across rivers, above paths, and elsewhere. It is believed that the prayers will be carried heavenward by the wind.

prayer wheel Hollow cylinder containing printed prayers. Every rotation equals a recitation of the contents. Prayer wheels come in all sizes, but most are handheld or hand-turned in fixed rows around temples, while some are turned by water or heat.

puja Prayer ceremony.

Rinpoche Title for reincarnate lamas and a name of respect given to Tibetan Buddhist teachers; literally, "great precious one."

sky burial Tibetan funeral custom in which the body is taken to a mountaintop and the flesh and bones are cut up, pulverized, and given to the birds.

stupa In Tibetan, called a *chorten,* an object for veneration; *stupa* literally means "heap" or "mound." It can be very small or massive, and is frequently used as a reliquary to contain different classes of relics including scriptures, blessed objects and even the bones of famous lamas.

sutra Sanskrit word for Buddhist scriptures—a discourse by the Buddha or a disciple—accepted as authoritative teaching. It can be a short sentence containing highly condensed teaching; literally, "a thread on which jewels are hung."

tantric Secret/mystical Buddhist practices involving mantras, rituals, and other esoteric practices.

Tara Most beloved of female Tibetan deities, Tara is the female aspect of Avalokiteshvara, and is considered the special protectress and savior of the Tibetan people. She symbolizes fertility and is believed to fulfill wishes.

thangka Tibetan iconographic scroll painting, usually done on cotton and framed by brocade.

tsampa Flour made from roasted and ground barley.

Tsang Westernmost of Tibet's two central provinces, known together as U-Tsang. Its chief city is Shigatse.

tsepon Government official analagous to the chancellor of the exchequer.

Tsong khapa (1357–1419) Great religious teacher and founder of Tibet's largest sect, the Gelugpas, popularly called the Yellow Hats.

vajra Scepterlike object in tantric ritual, symbolic of the indestructible nature of reality.

yidam Meditation deity on whom practitioners meditate to realize their own perfect qualities as that deity.

yogi One who undertakes a spiritual discipline or practice.

FERNS IN THE LOWER ELEVATIONS OF THE HIMALAYAS, PEMAYANGTSE, SIKKIM